First Edition Collectible

Genuine Autographed Collectible

10-Year Anniversary Edition

Thinking Especially of You
A Gift of Everlasting Love

Date:

To:

From:

Message:

"You don't marry someone you can live with.
You marry the person you cannot live without."
Unknown

The Cookbook of Everlasting Love

SEX ON A PLATE
FOOD AS FOREPLAY

10-Year Anniversary Edition

Dedication

To My Muse Cedric

"To the world you may be just one person,
but to one person you may be the world."
Brandi Snyder

Cookbook/Relationships/Love **10-YEAR ANNIVERSARY EDITION**

The Cookbook of Everlasting Love
SEX ON A PLATE: FOOD AS FOREPLAY

©2021 First Edition ©2010 by Sharon Esther Lampert. All Rights Reserved. No part of this book may be used or reproduced in any manner whatsoever without written permission except in the case of brief quotations embodied in critical articles and reviews.

KADIMAH PRESS books may be purchased for education, business, or sales promotional use.

KADIMAH PRESS
A Gift of Creative Genius

Book Website: www.TrueLoveBurnsEternal.com
Author Websites and Email:
www.SharonEstherLampert.com
www.PoetryJewels.com
www.WorldFamousPoems.com
Fans@SharonEstherLampert.com

Cover and Interior Book Design: Creative Genius Sharon Esther Lampert

Publisher: www.PalmBeachBookPublisher.com
Phone: 917-767-5843
Email: Sharon@PalmBeachBookPublisher.com

To Order Book:
Ingram, 1 Ingram Blvd. La Vergne, TN 37086-3629
Phone: 615-793-5000
Fax orders: 615-287-6990

Library of Congress Catalog Card Number: 2007924426
 ISBN Hardcover: 978-1-885872- 46-3
 ISBN Paperback: 978-1-885872- 48-7
 ISBN E-Book: 978-1-885872- 47-0
 UPC: 672180000035

Collector's Edition
Manufactured in the United States of America

10 YEAR ANNIVERSARY EDITION

The Cookbook of Everlasting Love

SEX ON A PLATE
FOOD AS FOREPLAY

Sharon Esther Lampert

KADIMAH PRESS
Gifts of Genius

True Love

True Love is Unconditional.
True Love is Found in the Deed.
True Love is Found in the We.
True Love Unites the Mind,
Body, and Heart as One.

Sharon Esther Lampert

*"Please Handle My Poems Gently.
These Poems Are My Remains."
Sharon Esther Lampert*

Contents

Aphrodite, the Greek Goddess of Sensuality
15

An Invitation to Dine: Love Has Arrived
19

Tokens of Affection and Pet Names
23

Figurative Toasts and Flirtatious Cocktails
29

Sultry and Seductive Champagnes
34

Classy Conversation Do's and Chummy Don'ts
36

Background Music in the Key of Love
39

Temptation Sample Menus
44

Matches Made in Heaven: Pairing Wine and Food
45

Whet Your Appetite: Tantalizing Spices

48

Amorous Appetizers

51

Vamp and Velvety Vinaigrettes

55

Ecstasy Entrees

57

Meat Melodies of Steamy Lust and Conquest

58

Poultry Ardor and Obsession

60

Games of Lust or Love

62

Fish Fantasy and Fixation

64

Pasta Infatuation or Addiction

66

Vegetarian Mania and Martyrdom

68

Erotic Side Dishes

71

Desserts of Seduction

77

Love Conquers All: Midnight Intercourses
85

Libido Lemonade to Maintain Sexual Stamina
89

Food As Foreplay: Erogenous Zones
91

A Romantic Kissy Brunch
93

A Goody Bag of Sweet Surrender
96

Conclusion: At Long Last, Love is Here to Stay
101

Special Treat: Say "I Love You" in Forty Languages
109

Song of Songs, Chapter 7, Biblical Love Poetry
110 English; 113 Hebrew

About the Author 114
True Love 9
That Kiss 70
No, I Don't Cook 78
My Man 100
Love Ever Reborn Is Love Ever Newborn 102
Shadayim 105
Remo: Drink, Drink, Drink 106
How to Read a Poem by Sharon Esther Lampert 117
Gifts of Poetry 118-120

Also By the Author 121
Fan Mail 124
Gratitude and Blessings 125

Aphrodite, the Greek Goddess of Sensuality

The Greek goddess of sensuality is Aphrodite, and the use of aphrodisiacs are believed to enhance sensuality.

"According to Greek poet Hesiod, she was born when Ouranos was castrated by his son Cronus. Cronus threw his severed genitals into the sea, and from the aphros (sea foam) arose Aphrodite. Hesiod's Theogony described that the genitals "were carried over the sea a long time, and white foam arose from the immortal flesh; with it a girl grew to become Aphrodite. It was said Aphrodite could make any man fall in love with her at their first sight of her" (Wikipedia, 2009).

Aphrodisiacs have existed for centuries, and studies have proven that many foods do have chemical components that elevate mood, and even create the sensation of falling in love. Some foods are considered aphrodisiacs because they are chemical stimulents, such as oysters and chocolate. Some foods are considered aphrodisiacs because they have a phallic shape, such as bananas and asparagus. Some foods are considered aphrodisiacs for there arousing aroma, such as vanilla and honey. Here is the official list of world renown aphrodisiacs that have been used for centuries as libido boosters to enhance sexual desire.

The Classic Culinary Aphrodisiacs

Aphrodite was born from the sea, and many types of seafood have reputations as aphrodisiacs.

Oysters are a classic culinary aphrodisiac. Oysters are loaded with zinc, a key nutrient for testosterone production and stimulates the libido in both men and women. Oysters are a lean source of protein, and have been credited with keeping men virile (before Viagra). According to popular legend, Cassanova ate more than 50 oysters every morning to help him stay in top form. As a matter of fact, we know that bodybuilders consume more than 50 egg whites on a daily basis to keep themselves in top form, so this is not that far-fetched or stretched a tale.

Caviar is a classic culinary aphrodisiac. It is high in zinc, which stimulates the formation of testosterone, maintaining male functionality. The tactile sensation of the black pearls bursting against the tongue is a legal "drug of choice." All eggs are associated with new life and caviar, "fish eggs" are no exception. Eggs are considered the ultimate symbol of fertility for many ancient nations, e.g., Easter and Passover. Three specific species of sturgeon indigenous to the

Caspian Sea are Sevruga, Osetra and Beluga; and these fish eggs are the most-prized caviar in the world. In 2006, the United Nations put a temporary ban on Caspian Sea caviar because the, Beluga, the most prized of the three caviar, were near extinction. Today, a world leader in sustainable sturgeon farming is the aquafarm of, Tsar Nicoulai caviar, in Northern California. The hard-to-get, high-priced, and near-extinction caviar is the ultimate aphrodisiac because playing hard-to-get has always been sexy.

Truffles, black or white, are classic culinary aphrodisiacs. The rarer black truffle has the most concentrated potency. The scent of the male pheromone andostrenone is replicated by the truffles' musky scent and stimulates the libido. Truffles were a legendary aphrodisiac of ancient Rome. Centuries later, it was noted that, Napoleon, ate truffles to increase his masculine potency. According to popular folklore, during a wedding feast, a groom would gorge on Alba truffles to sustain his masculinity.

Pomegranates are a classic culinary aphrodisiac. The Bible has many references to this fruit and it is still playing a starring role in contemporary society. The pomegranate is respected the world over for its beautiful color, delicious taste, and health benefits. Although it is a chore to break open and eat, it is considered one of the best sources of antioxidants. In the Orient, pomegranates are used to treat depression, settle upset stomachs, and neutralize internal parasites.

Goji Berries are a classic culinary aphrodisiac in China. For centuries in Asia, goji berries are referred to as the "happy berries." They are administered to strengthen the adrenal system, believed to be a center of sexual energy. They claim to have the highest content of beta-carotene of all fruits.

Chocolate is a classic culinary aphrodisiac. The Aztecs and Mayans considered it a luxury with aphrodisiac powers, and referred to chocolate as "nourishment of the Gods." According to popular folklore, the Mayans used cacao beans to pay for prostitutes (The going rate was around eight beans per woman). And the great Aztec ruler, Montezuma, consumed as much as 50 cups of chocolate elixir before heading off to his harem. As of today, we know that chocolate contains antioxidants, namely, flavonoids.

Honey is a classic culinary aphrodisiac. According to popular folklore, newly wed couples would drink mead (a fermented drink made from honey) on their "honeymoon" to "sweeten" the marriage.

The Classic Phallic Shape Aphrodisiacs:

Shark is a classic culinary aphrodisiac in China. The fish's dorsal fin is the aphrodisiac because it contains 21 grams of energy-sustaining protein, magnesium, and selenium, an important nutrient for sperm production.

Bananas are a classic culinary aphrodisiac in India. To this very day, bananas are included in Indian offerings to the fertility gods. In Islam, bananas were believed to be the forbidden fruit of the Garden of Eden. In the Caribbean and Central America, the sap of the red banana tree is sipped as an aphrodisiac elixir. Bananas are packed with potassium and B vitamins that are essential for the production of sexual hormones. They also contain an enzyme bromelain that may enhance male performance. Bananas have a phallic shape and creamy lush texture that exudes sex appeal.

Asparagus is a classic culinary aphrodisiac. According to popular folklore, three courses of asparagus were served to 19th century bridegrooms due to its reputed aphrodisiacal powers. Asparagus is a phallic symbol that is high in vitamin E which stimulates hormones. These phytohormones mimic steroid-like action.

Chilies are a culinary aphrodisiac. They have a a phallic shape and are a mood enhancing chemical stimulent. The chemical capsaicin triggers a release of endorphins.

"Sow Your Wild Oats"

Wild Oats are a classic culinary aphrodisiac. They are rich in B vitamins and a good source of fiber. In China, green oats have been used for centuries as a treatment for low libido. In Anglo-Saxon homeopathy, they were used to treat female infertility. Olympic athletes reportedly begin their day with steel cut oats "high-octane fuel" for a productive workout.

Champagne is a classic culinary aphrodisiac. It is a symbol of celebration in many parts of the world Champagne hits the blood stream more quickly than wine. The steady stream of delicate bubbles wraps the mind, heart, and body in a warm glow of intoxication. It is considered the "drink of love."

An Invitation to Dine: Love Has Arrived

Set the Mood for an Intimate Romantic Dinner
Before you embark on a romantic journey, you need to have the intimate details of your loved one at your fingertips, to make every step count towards bringing you closer to finding your true love: Establish a connection, enhance compatibility, recognize common ground, and develop a relationship based on the fulfillment of mutual needs.

Q: What is your loved one's favorite color?
A: For tablecloth, flowers, love notes, bathrobe, toothbrush, bathroom towels, and sheets

Q: What is your loved one's favorite type of music?
A: Classical, Broadway show tunes, rock, or pop?

Q: What is your loved one's favorite food?
A: Chicken, beef, duck, fish, or vegetarian?

Q: Do you have any allergies?
A: Nuts, fruits, flowers, bedding detergents, cats

Q: What is your loved one's favorite dessert?
A: Cake, pie, cookies, or cheese plate?

Q: What is your loved one's favorite breakfast?
A: French toast, pancakes, muffins, eggs, or oatmeal?

Prepare the Dining Area
Create a magical mood for your loved one by mixing the right ingredients for romance:
1. Dim the lights
2. Set the table with candles
3. Set the mood with music in the key of love (p. 39)
4. Set the table with flowers
5. Set the plate with a token of affection (p. 24)
6. Write a hand-written love note: Poetry preferred (p. 23)
7. Make a space to dance to a favorite song before dessert is served
8. Have a camera on hand to record all of your wonderful memories

Preparations for a Romantic Bathroom

1. Designate the bathroom towels as His and Hers

2. Buy an extra toothbrush in the right color for you loved one

3. Place a bottle of bubbles in the bathroom; test out the bubbles, because it is disappointing if the bathtub does not fill up with big-foaming bubbles

4. Place a bottle of massage oil and moisturizer in the bathroom; test the smell of the massage oil and moisturizer for products that are not overly feminine or masculine

5. Laminate the lyrics to a popular love song duet, so that you can both sit in the bathtub and sing the romantic song (copy shops have lamination machines)

6. Spray perfume or cologne on the bedding

7. Put a photo of the two of you in a frame and place it on the dresser by the bed

Preparations for a Romantic Bedroom

Make a space in your heart, in your bed, in your dresser, and in your closet. Empty a drawer, designate that draw as His or Hers, and and fill it with the following essentials:
1. Contraception
2. Shampoo, hair brush, and hair dryer
3. Shaving cream, razor, and aftershave
4. Contact lense solution and a case for the lenses
5. Extra pair of underwear and socks or pantyhose
6. Beautiful lingerie or cozy pajamas
7. A handwritten love note sprayed with perfume
8. Place hangers in the closet as His and Hers by placing a bow on the hangers
9. If you have a cat, make sure you have a special cat hair-removal roller available
10. Prepare another wallet-sized photo for your loved one's wallet
11. An alarm clock that wakes you up to the sound of music

Tokens of Affection and Pet Names

Write a love note and place it in the center of the plate. Feed the emotional hunger of your loved one first by filling the heart with love before you feed the body with a homecooked meal made with love. It is well worth your time and effort to send an exceptional handwritten note to a loved one, because personalized love notes are saved and passed down for future generations, and published in books. Phone calls have a short life span and emails are too impersonal. These eight ground rules also apply for sending out an after dinner thank you note.

1. Use attractive stationary in your loved one's favorite color

2. Write a handwritten note and use a pen with black ink

3. Address your sweetheart with a pet name, e.g. Dear Sugarball

4. Write a rough draft of the note on scratch paper to sort out all of your feelings, organize your thoughts, and correct your typos

5. Express your heartfelt feelings in 1-5 sentences

6. Sign the note with a pet name, e.g., Your Stud Muffin

7. Spray perfume or cologne on the envelope

8. If you are composing an after dinner thank you note, send it out the very next day

Pet Names for a Loved One:

For Him:
Teddybear
Sweetcheeks
Dreamboat
Heartthrob
Lovebird
Casanova
Don Juan
Shnookums
Cupcake

For Her:
Sunshine
Sugarplum
Sweet Potato
Babycake
Honey Bunny
Angel Face
Pumpkin
Sweetie Pie
Lovedove

From Bed to Wed, Never Visit a Loved One Empty-handed

The First Token of Affection
A single rose and a hand-written love note

The Second Token of Affection
A box of chocolates and a hand-written love note

The Third Token of Affection
A favorite CD and a hand-written love note

The Fourth Token of Affection
A teddybear and and a hand-written love note

The Fifth Token of Affection
A favorite book and a hand-written love note

The Sixth Token of Affection
Make a scrapbook of photographs taken of the two of you enjoying life

The Seventh Token of Affection
A gift certificate for a favorite store and a hand-written note
For women: Jewelry or sexy lingerie
For men: Cologne, sporting goods, watch, tie clip, cufflinks

The Ground Rules for Tokens of Affection
Here are four ground rules for tokens of affection:

Your Face:
1. On your face, you should wear a big smile

Your Heart:
2. Your heart needs to be full of warm compliments

Your Hands:
3. In your hands, there should be a personalized gift accompanied by a handwritten note
4. Attach a small piece of candy or chocolate bar to the gift and love note

The Love Notes:

Here are some classic love notes by known and unknown writers, that are loved by all, and passed down through the generations:

Seduce my mind and you can have my body. Find my soul and I'm yours forever.
- Anonymous

In the arithmetic of love, one plus one equals everything, and two minus one equals nothing. – Anonymous

Fortune and love befriend the bold. – By Ovid

Life is the flower for which love is the honey. – By Victor Hugo

I don't wish to be everything to everyone, but I would like to be something to someone.
– By Javan

Gravitation can not be held responsible for people falling in love. – By Albert Einstein

Where there is love, there is life. - By Gandhi

Love isn't blind; it just only sees what matters.
- By William Curry

The Love Notes:

Who being loved, is poor? - By Oscar Wilde

There is a miracle that happens every time to those who really love; the more they give, the more they possess."
- By Rainer Maria Rilke

What a grand thing, to be loved! What a grander thing still, to love. - By Victor Hugo

There is only one happiness in life: to love and be loved. - By George Sand

Since love grows within you, so beauty grows. For love is the beauty of the soul.
- By St. Augustine

I only wish to be the fountain of love, From which you drink, Every drop promising eternal passion.
~ Anonymous

Only love let's us see normal things in an extraordinary way. -Anonymous

Love is not a matter of counting the years...
But making the years count.
-By Michelle St. Amand

Love is smiling on the inside and out. - By Jennifer Williams

The Love Notes:

You don't love a woman because she's beautiful, She is beautiful because you love her.
~ Anonymous

A heart that loves is always young. -A Greek Proverb

I have found men who didn't know how to kiss.
I've always found time to teach them.
- By Mae West

It is not the men in my life, it is the life in my men.
- By Mae West

You will never know true happiness
until you have truly loved,
and you will never understand
what pain really is
until you have lost it.
~ Anonymous

You don't find love, you create love.
- Sharon Esther Lampert

There is no such thing as too much love.
- Sharon Esther Lampert

True Love

True Love is Unconditional.
True Love is Found in the Deed.
True Love is Found in the We.
True Love Unites the Mind,
Body, and Heart as One.
- By Sharon Esther Lampert

Figurative Toasts and Flirtatious Cocktails

Toasts are appropriate anytime friends get together socially and alcoholic drinks are served. Prepare your toasts beforehand and memorize them. There are five ground rules for creating memorable toasts.

1. Say what is in your heart.

2. Keep it simple, short, and to the point because simplicity equals sincerity (1-2 sentences). Save your long-winded joke or story for after dessert.

3. Who is your audience? Are you toasting a first date, a lover, or a life partner?

4. Be poetic. Use rhythm and rhyme to deliver a memorable toast.

5. Use surprise. As your relationship grows, change your toast to reflect the deepening affection. Don't be repetitive and boring.

The First Toast
The first toast is offered before eating and serves to welcome your guest:

1. This toast celebrates you (insert name).

2. Thank you (insert name) for joining me for dinner.

The Second Toast
The second toast is made after dessert when the wine glasses are refilled. Here are some classic toasts by unknown writers, that are loved by all, and passed down through the generations:

1. May all your joys be pure joys, and all your pain champagne.

2. I have known many, liked not a few, loved only one, I toast to you.

3. May you both live as long as you want, and never want as long as you live.

4. Coming together is a beginning; keeping together is progress; working together is success.

5. May your troubles be less and your blessings be more.
   And nothing but happiness come through your door.

End Your Toast with a Traditional Greetings:

America: Cheers

Australia: Cheers

Arabic: Fisehatak

Canada: Cheers

China: Gan bei

French: Santé

Hebrew: L'chaim

Hungarian: Egészsegunkre

Gaelic: Sláinte

German: Prost

India: A la sature

Italian: Salute

Japan: Kampai

Latin: Sanitas bona

Russian: Budem zdorovy

Tagalog: Mabuhay

Zulu: Oogy wawa

Flirtatious Cocktails

Love Potion 8: Kiss Me You Fool

Ingredients:
6 oz chilled Champagne
2 oz triple sec
6 oz cranberry juice

Instructions:
Stir ingredients together in a champagne glass, and serve

Love Potion 11: Kiss Me Tenderly

Ingredients:
1.5 oz vodka
11 oz Champagne
0.5 oz Blue Curacao liqueur

Instructions:
1. Pour the vodka into a sugar-rimmed champagne flute
2. Fill the rest of the glass with Champagne
3. Top with the Curacao, and serve

Love Potion 22: Kiss Me All Over

Ingredients:
6 oz Champagne
2 oz cherry brandy
2 oz sugar
2 tsp orange juice

Instructions:
1. Pour the cherry brandy and orange juice over the sugar in a champagne flute
2. Add the champagne, and serve
3. Garnish with a slice of orange

Love Potion 40: Kiss Me, Miss Me, and Never Diss Me

Pineapple Champagne Cocktail

Ingredients:

6 oz Champagne

4 pieces fresh pineapples

1 oz Cointreau® orange liqueur

1 oz vodka

2 oz pineapple juice

Instructions:

1. Add the pineapple pieces and cointreau in the bottom of a mixing glass
2. Add vodka and pineapple juice and stir
3. Strain into a chilled cocktail glass and top with champagne
4. Garnish with a cherry, and serve

Love Potion 69: Kiss and Don't Ever Tell

Raspberry Champagne Cocktail

Ingredients:

3/4 cup chilled Champagne

3/4 teaspoon Chambord (raspberry-flavored liqueur)

Instructions: Combine Chambord and Champagne in a flute

Love Potion 88: Kiss Only Me Forever

Pear Champagne Cocktail

Ingredients:

1/2 ounce pear cognac, such as, Belle de Brillet

Splash of Grand Marnier

Garnish with lemon twist

Instructions:

1. Pour 1/2 ounce pear cognac into a fluted glass
2. Fill with chilled champagne
3. Top off with a splash of Grand Marnier
4. Garnish with a pear slice or lemon twist

Sultry and Seductive Champagnes

Champagne is made only from the grapes that are grown and cultivated in the vineyards of the Champagne region of France. Champagne is made from mixing, blending, and harmonizing three grape varieties, Pinot Noir, Chardonnay, and Pinot Meunier. Each grape contributes a special character that when blended together create a unique symphony of fragrant and fanciful flavors.

Light Bodied
- Laurent-Perrier
- Perrier-Jouët
- Taittinger

Medium Bodied
- Charles Heidsieck
- Deutz
- Joseph Perrier
- Moët & Chandon (Dom Perignon)
- Mumm
- Philipponnat
- Piper-Heidsieck
- Pol Roger
- Pommery

Full Bodied
- Bollinger
- Delamotte
- Gosset
- Heidsieck Monopole
- Henriot
- Krug
- Louis Roederer (Cristal)
- Vueve Clicquot

Champagnes Vary
- Extra Brut (Brut Sauvage) - Totally dry
- Brut - Dry
- Extra Dry - Medium dry
- Sec - Slightly sweet
- Demi - Sec: Fairly sweet
- Doux - Sweet

Classy Conversation Do's and Chummy Dont's

Prepare Your Talking Points Beforehand: Feed Heart and Soul
- Compliments on appearance
- Laugh-out-loud oneliners
- Stick to areas of common ground and compatibility
- Movies, museum exhibits, concerts, and books

Do's
- Live in the moment and celebrate life
- Stay focused on the person in front of you
- Keep notes on that person's interests
- Enjoy the other person's company
- When silence is deafening, read poetry (see appendix: "Immortality Is Mine")
- Let intimate conversation build slowly and naturally
- Build wonderful memories together and record them on camera
- Establish pet names for each other

Don'ts
A dinner date is not a therapy session. Work out your personal and work-related problems with a professional (keep a self-reflection journal)

Topics of Conversation that Are Off the Table
- Don't talk about problems at work
- Don't talk about your personal problems: Addictions, compulsions, and idiosyncrasies
- Don't talk about your old flames
- Don't talk about your imperfect past
- Don't talk about politics or religion
- Don't gossip about other people
- Don't say you had a perfect childhood (no such thing)
- Don't interview your date by asking a hundred personal questions
- Don't tell racially sensitive jokes

Background Music in the Key of Love

Almost every other song ever written is a love song. Love songs vary from unrequited love, to romantic love, to consuming love, to lost love and broken-hearted love. Any list of love songs gathered is a short list and is incomplete. The best list of happy love songs are the ones that are sung at weddings, when a couple steps out onto the dance floor as a married couple.

1. Ask your loved one for a music preference. Download the song from iTunes. Laminate the lyrics of the song and place it in the center of the plate with a handwritten love note.

2. Choose ten to twenty love songs from the following lists of classical and popular music. The best way to collect great romantic music is to download the songs individually on iTunes into your computer, then load them into your iPod, and turn your iPod into a stereo.
   a. Don't play the same song over and over again
   b. Vary the songs by male and female vocals
   c. Choose an appropriate set of songs for cocktails, dinner, dessert, and lovemaking

Here are recommendations for classical background music in the key of love:

Classical Music: The Romantic Composers

1. Arensky, Anton — Russian, (1861-1906)
2. Beethoven, Ludwig van — German, (1770-1827)
3. Berlioz, Hector — French, (1803-1869)
4. Brahms, Johannes — German, (1833-1897)
5. Borodin, Alexandr — Russian, (1833-1887)
6. Bruckner, Anton — Austrian, (1824-1896)
7. Chopin, Fréderic — Polish, (1810-1849)
8. Debussy, Claude — French, (1862-1918)
9. Dvořák, Antonin — Czech, (1841-1904)
10. Elgar, Edward — English, (1857-1934)
11. Fauré, Gabriel — French, (1845-1924)
12. Franck, César — French, (1822-1890)
13. Glazunov, Alexander — Russian, (1865-1936)
14. Glinka, Mikhail — Russian, (1804-1857)
15. Grieg, Edvard — Norwegian, (1843-1907)
16. Liszt, Franz — Hungarian, (1811-1886)
17. Mahler, Gustav — Austrian, (1860-1911)
18. Mendelssohn, Felix — German, (1809-1847)
19. Rachmaninoff, Sergei — Russian, (1873-1943)
20. Ravel, Maurice — French, (1875-1937)
21. Saint-Saëns, Camille — French, (1835-1921)
22. Schubert, Franz — Austrian, (1797-1828)
23. Schumann, Robert — German, (1810-1856)
24. Sibelius, Jean — Finnish, (1865-1957)
25. Smetana, Bedrich — Czech, (1824-1884)
26. Tchaikovsky, Peter Ilyich — Russian, (1840-1893)
27. Verdi, Giuseppe — Italian, (1813-1901)
28. Wagner, Richard — German, (1813-1883)

Here is a list of popular love songs for background music in the key of love:

1. The Greatest Love of All - Whitney Houston
2. Because You Loved Me - Celine Dion
3. Unchained Melody - The Righteous Brothers
4. Wind Beneath My Wings - Bette Midler
5. Endless Love - Lionel Ritchie
6. A Thousand Miles - Vanessa Carlton
7. All My Life - K.C. and JoJo
8. Faithfully - Journey
9. Now And Forever - Richard Marx
10. Here And Now - Luther Vandross
11. Always and Forever - Kenny Rogers
12. One Love - Bob Marley
13. Up Where We Belong - Joe Cocker and Jennifer Warnes
14. Your Song - Elton John
15. Lady In Red - Chris De Burgh
16. Amazed - Lonestar
17. Baby I Love Your Way - Peter Frampton
18. Baby, Baby - Amy Grant
19. Wonderufl Tonight - Eric Clapton
20. Breathe - Faith Hill
21. When I Think About Angels - Jamie O'Neal
22. Forever And For Always - Shania Twain
23. When I Fall In Love - Nat King Cole
24. Secret Garden - Bruce Springsteen
25. For You I Will - Monica
26. Always On My Mind - Elvis Presley
27. Fly Me To The Moon - Frank Sinatra
28. Truly Madly Deeply - Savage Garden
29. Beautiful - James Blunt
30. When I Fall In Love With You - Carpenters
31. More Than Words - Extreme
32. As Long As You Love Me - Backstreet Boys
33. When A Man Loves A Woman - Percy Sledge
34. Beautiful In My Eyes - Joshua Kadison
35. Can't Help Falling In Love - Julio Iglesias
36. I Could Fall In Love - Selena

37. Keep On Loving You - Reo Speedwagon
38. Vision Of Love - Mariah Carey
39. Hero - Enrique Iglesias
40. Back At One - Brian McKnight
41. Crazy For You - Madonna
42. Have I Told You Lately - Rod Stewart
43. Tonight I Celebrate My Love - Peabo Bryson and Roberta Flack
44. Groovy Kind Of Love - Phil Collins
45. I Knew I Loved You - Savage Garden
46. Can You Feel The Love Tonight - Elton John
47. Somewhere Out There - James Ingram and Linda Ronstadt
48. Here In My Heart - Martina Mcbride
49. From This Moment On - Shania Twain
50. Body And Soul - Tony Bennett
51. If You Are Not The One - Daniel Bedingfield
52. Someday We'll Know - Mandy Moore
53. Unforgettable - Natalie Cole f/ Nat King Cole
54. You're Still The One - Shania Twain
55. I Melt With You - Modern English
56. Your Body Is A Wonderland - John Mayer
57. Crash - Dave Matthews Band
58. I'll Be - Edwin McCain
59. Don't Wanna Miss A Thing - Aerosmith
60. Nothing Compares 2 U - Sinead O'Conner
61. All I Want Is You - U2
62. I Do - 98 Degrees
63. A Whole New World - Alladin
64. Sexual Healing - Marvin Gaye
65. Always Be My Baby - Mariah Carey
66. Angel in Your Eyes - John Michael Montgomery
67. At Last - Etta James
68. Back To You - John Mayer
69. Beauty and the Beast - Celine Dion
70. Beautiful Soul - Jesse McCartney
71. I Need You - LeAnn Rimes
72. Come What May - Nicole Kidman, Ewan McGregor
73. Don't Wanna Lose You - Gloria Estefan
74. Everything I Do - Bryan Adams
75. Fever - Joe Cocker

Temptation Sample Menus

First Date

Flirtatious Cocktail: Love Potion 8: Kiss Me You Fool
Amorous Appetizer: Guileless Goat Cheese Stuffed Roasted Figs
Ecstasy Entree: Femme Fatale Meat Loaf with Flirty Red Peppers and Sex Kitten Onions
Erotic Side Dish: Hunk of Burning Love Sweet Potatoes
Decadent Dessert: To Die For Chocolate Almond Torte and a Rainbow of Sun-Kissed Berries
Inter-Course: Sex Kitten Chocolate Dipped Strawberries and Pink Lemonade
Kissy Breakfast: Addicted to Love Cheese Blinzes
A Goody Bag of Sweet Surrender: Casanova Chocolate Marshmellow Fudge

Going Steady

Flirtatious Cocktail: Love Potion 69: Kiss and Don't Ever Tell
Amorous Appetizer: Gorgeous Smoked Salmon Cucumber Sandwiches
Ecstasy Entree: Crush-Crazy Chicken with Amour Artichokes, and Sultry Sundried Tomatoes
Erotic Side Dish: Orgasmic Corn with Climactic Red, Green, and Yellow Peppers
Decadent Dessert: Princess Kadimah's Ethereal Brownies and Sorbet
Inter-Course: Sex Kitten Chocolate Dipped Pineapples and Blueberry Lemonade
Kissy Breakfast: Voluptuous Lemon Buttermilk Blueberry Pancakes
A Goody Bag of Sweet Surrender: Salome Chocolate-Cognac-Almond Truffles

Engaged

Flirtatious Cocktail: Love Potion 22: Kiss Me All Over
Amorous Appetizer: Love Is Blini with Caviar and Crème Fraîche
Ecstasy Entree: Sultry and Slinky Red Snapper with Ginger-Garlic-Sesame Infusion and Scallions
Erotic Side Dish: Mata Hari Barley Risotto With Asparagus and Parmesan
Decadent Dessert: Dream Boat Creamy Cheesecake
Inter-Course: Sex Bomb Chocolate Marshmellows and Water Melon Lemonade
Kissy Breakfast: Love Drenched Challah French Toast
A Goody Bag of Sweet Surrender: Cleopatra Chocolate Hazelnut Biscotti

Matches Made in Heaven: Pairing Wine and Food

How to Read a Wine Label?
If I see a beautiful wine label, I buy the wine. Most people don't buy wine this way. Here is how wine connoisseurs buy a bottle of wine:

1. Vintage
Wine is meant to be drunk right away, so make sure the wine is not old.

2. Alcohol Content
Make sure the alcohol content is 14% and below. Too much alcohol creates an "unbalanced" wine.

3. Geography
Famous vineyards produce high-quality grapes. If the label gives a specific location, it is usually a clue that the wine is of higher quality.

4. Estate-bottled
This means that the vineyard that grew the grapes made the wine.

Pairing Wine with Food
1. Red or White?
Most of us grew up hearing white wine with white meat, chicken and fish, and red wine with red meat and pasta, however, this rule can be broken.

2. Heavy or Light?
Think about the weight and complexity of food: Lighter with lighter and heavier with heavier

3. What Are the Six Culinary Tastes?
Seasoning -- spices, herbs, and citrus --create the five tastes of sweet, salty, sour, pungent and bitter. The Japanese introduced a sixth taste, umami, which relates to raw fish, oysters, and mushrooms.

Cabernet Sauvignon
Foods: Blue cheese, beef, veal, lamb, red pasta sauce, strong cheese, dark chocolate

Chardonnay
Foods: Cream/white sauces, poultry, salmon, veal, crab, scallops

Chenin Blanc
Foods: Shellfish, poultry, Asian food

Chianti
Foods: Red meat, pork, red pasta sauces, poultry

Gewurztraminer
Foods: Spicy Asian food, pork, poultry

Merlot
Foods: Red meat, salmon, pasta, game meat

Pinot Gris
Foods: Fruit, shellfish, cheese, cream sauces, red sauces, poultry

Pinot Noir
Foods: Poultry, game meat, tomato sauce, strong cheese

Rieslings
Foods: Spicy dishes, most Asian food, crab, fruit, poultry and fish

Sauvignon Blanc
Foods: Fish, seafood, lighter pastas, salads, poultry

Syrah or Shiraz
Foods: Beef, poultry, salmon, stronger cheeses

Zinfandel (red)
Foods: Game meat, barbecued meat, tomato sauce for pasta

Zinfandel (white)
Foods: Asian food, chicken, pork

Whet Your Appetite: Tantalizing Spices

*"His cheeks are as a bed of spices, as sweet flowers:
his lips like lilies, dropping sweet smelling myrrh."*
Song of Solomon, 5:13

The following flavor and food combinations, make meat, poultry, fish and vegetables delicious and nutritious without the addition of salt or sugar.

For meat, poultry and fish, try one or more of these combinations:

Beef: Bay leaf, marjoram, nutmeg, onion, pepper, sage, thyme
Lamb: Curry powder, garlic, rosemary, mint
Pork: Garlic, onion, sage, pepper, oregano
Veal: Bay leaf, curry powder, ginger, marjoram, oregano
Chicken: Ginger, marjoram, oregano, paprika, poultry seasoning, rosemary, sage, tarragon, thyme
Fish: Curry powder, dill, dry mustard, marjoram, paprika, pepper

For vegetables, experiment with one or more of these combinations:

Carrots: Cinnamon, cloves, dill, ginger, marjoram, nutmeg, rosemary, sage
Corn: Cumin, curry powder, onion, paprika, parsley
Green Beans: Dill, curry powder, marjoram, oregano, tarragon, thyme
Greens: Onion, pepper
Potatoes: Dill, garlic, onion, paprika, parsley, sage
Summer Squash: Cloves, curry powder, marjoram, nutmeg, rosemary, sage
Winter Squash: Cinnamon, ginger, nutmeg, onion
Tomatoes: Basil, bay leaf, dill, marjoram, onion, oregano, parsley, pepper

Reducing Sugar:
Reduce or eliminate sugar by using sweet-tasting spices
Allspice, Anise, Cardamom, Cinnamon, Cloves, Ginger, Mace, Nutmeg

"I don't wish to be everything to everyone,
but I would like to be something to someone."
Javan

"The Most Important Relationship Is The One You Have with Yourself!
Your Lover Is **BONUS LOVE!**"

Sharon Esther Lampert

Amorous Appetizers

"One cannot think well, love well, sleep well, if one has not dined well."
Virgina Woolf

Guileless Goat Cheese Stuffed Roasted Figs

Ingredients:
12 figs, Goat cheese, and honey

Preparation:
1. Quarter 12 figs, cutting three-quarters of the way down
2. Stuff the figs with goat cheese
3. Roast in an oiled pan at 425° for 12 minutes, until softened
4. Serve drizzled with warmed honey

Gorgeous Smoked Salmon Cucumber Sandwiches

Main Ingredients:
3 ounces sliced smoked salmon or lox
3 slices thin Danish pumpernickel bread
12 thin slices English hothouse cucumber
2 tablespoons (1/4 stick) unsalted butter (room temperature)

Spices:
1 teaspoon minced fresh dill
3/4 teaspoon Dijon mustard
Freshly ground pepper
Fresh dill sprigs

Preparation:
1. Mix butter, dill, and mustard in a small bowl
2. Spread bread with butter mixture
3. Cover with cucumber slices, then salmon
4. Sprinkle with pepper
5. Cut each sandwich into 4 triangles
6. Top each with dill sprig and serve

Amorous Appetizers

Love Is Blini with Caviar and Crème Fraîche

Main Ingredients:
1/4 cup whole wheat flour
1/2 cup buckwheat flour
 (use whole wheat flour if buckwheat is unavailable)
2 cups sifted all-purpose flour
1 cup milk
3 eggs, separated
4 to 6 ounces caviar
1 pint crème fraîche

Kitchen Cabinet Ingredients:
1 1/4 teaspoons active dry yeast
1 teaspoon sugar
1 cup warm water
1/2 teaspoon salt
2 tablespoons unsalted butter, melted
Vegetable oil for frying

Cooking Instructions:

Prepare the Dough

1. Combine whole wheat flour, buckwheat flour, 1 cup of the all-purpose flour, the yeast, sugar and warm water

2. Cover tightly with plastic wrap and let stand in a warm place until doubled in volume (1 to 1 1/2 hours)

3. In a saucepan, scald the milk by cooking it to just under a boil; let cool to room temperature and set aside

4. Whisk together the egg yolks and salt until light in texture and color; then gradually whisk in the butter until smooth

5. Stir in the scalded milk, then stir in the remaining 1 cup all-purpose flour until smooth; fold in the flour mixture (step 1) until the batter is smooth

6. Cover tightly with plastic wrap and let stand in a warm place to rise (30 to 40 minutes)

7. Using a whisk, beat the egg whites until stiff peaks form

8. Using a spatula, gently fold the egg whites into the batter and let stand (10 to 12 minutes)

9. In a large nonstick fry pan or griddle over medium heat, warm just enough oil to coat the bottom of the pan; cook until golden (2 to 3 minutes per side)

10. Serve the blini with crème fraîche and caviar

Amorous Appetizers

Sweet Potato Latkes with Applesauce

Main Ingredients:
2 cups grated raw potatoes
1 cup grated sweet potatoes
1/4 cup finely sliced and chopped leeks
garnish, sourcream or applesauce

Kitchen Cabinet Ingredients:
2 large eggs
1 tsp salt
1/4 cup dry breadcrumbs or crackers
freshly-ground black pepper to taste

Cooking Instructions:
Prepare the Potatoes
1. Peel and grate three large potatoes in a bowl
2. Use a sieve to remove the excess water to obtain finely grated potatoes, about 2 cups
3. Combine the chopped leeks, eggs, breadcrumbs, salt and pepper, mix thoroughly, and add to potatoes
4. Bake in an oven or fry in a skillet (traditional method)

To Bake in an Oven:
1. Preheat the oven to 400 degrees
2. Spray a baking pan with a thin coat of canola oil
3. Drop heaping spoonfuls of the mixture onto the pan
4. Shape and flatten them out with the back of the spoon
5. Make the latkes in 4-inch rounds and about ¾ inch thick
6. Bake until golden brown with crispy edges (20-30 minutes)
7. Serve piping hot with garnish: Sourcream or applesauce

To Fry in a Skillet:
1. In a large heavy skillet, melt butter and vegetable oil to a depth of about ¼ inch
2. Use a large spoon to drop the pancake mixture in the oil
3. Flatten the mixture and fry until golden brown, turning once
4. Drain and serve piping hot with garnish: Sourcream or applesauce

Amorous Appetizers

Va Va Voom Spinach Salad
with Feta Cheese, Pecans, and Dried Cherries

The Salad Ingredients:

2 bags (6 oz. each) baby spinach
1/2 cup crumbled Feta cheese
1/2 cup dried cherries
1/2 cup sliced natural pecans

Prepare the Salad:

1. Place the spinach in a large salad bowl
2. Top with the Feta cheese, dried cherries, and pecans
3. Cover and refrigerate until serving
4. Add vinaigrette of choice

Strapping Roquefort Cheese Stud Salad
with Arugula, Pears, and Walnuts

The Salad Ingredients:

2 bags (6 oz. each) Arugula
1/2 cup crumbled Roquefort cheese
1/2 cup sliced pears
1/2 cup sliced natural walnuts

Prepare the Salad:

1. Place the Arugula in a large salad bowl
2. Top with the Roquefort cheese, pears, and walnuts
3. Cover and refrigerate until serving
4. Add vinaigrette of choice

Vamp and Velvety Vinaigrettes

Whisk all ingredients together for 1 1/4 cups
The vinaigrette will keep, tightly covered, for a week in the refrigerator

Champagne Vinaigrette
1 shallot, peeled and quartered
1/4 cup champagne vinegar or white-wine vinegar
1/4 cup extra-virgin olive oil
1 tablespoon Dijon mustard
3/4 teaspoon salt
Freshly ground pepper to taste

Raspberry Vinaigrette
1/3 cup canola oil
1/4 cup raspberry vinegar or red-wine vinegar
3 tablespoons orange juice
1/4 teaspoon salt
Freshly ground pepper to taste

Walnut-Lemon Vinaigrette
2 tablespoons walnut oil
1 tablespoon minced shallot
1/4 teaspoon freshly grated lemon zest
1 tablespoon lemon juice
1 teaspoon whole-grain or Dijon mustard
1/4 teaspoon salt
Freshly ground pepper to taste

Maple-Mustard Vinaigrette
1/2 cup walnut or canola oil
1/4 cup maple syrup
1/4 cup cider vinegar
2 tablespoons coarse-grained mustard
2 tablespoons soy sauce
1/2 teaspoon salt
1/2 teaspoon pepper

Cilantro-Lime Vinaigrette
1 cup packed cilantro
1/2 cup extra-virgin olive oil
1/4 cup lime juice
1/4 cup orange juice
1/2 teaspoon salt
1/2 teaspoon pepper
Pinch of minced garlic

Mustard-Chive Vinaigrette
1 tablespoon grainy Dijon-style mustard
1/4 cup finely chopped fresh chives
2 tablespoons white vinegar
1 tablespoon water
2 teaspoons honey
1/4 teaspoon salt
4 tablespoons olive oil (add slowly at end)
Add freshly ground black pepper to taste

Mustard-Olive Balsamic Vinaigrette
1/2 cup balsamic vinegar
1/4 cup extra-virgin olive oil
1/4 cup canola oil
2 tablespoons coarse-grained mustard
12 Kalamata olives, pitted and finely chopped
1 tablespoon maple syrup or
1 1/2 teaspoons brown sugar
1 teaspoon dried basil

Citrus Vinaigrette
1/4 cup fresh orange juice (juice of one small orange)
1/4 cup fresh lemon juice
2 tablespoons olive oil
2 tablespoons canola oil
1/2 teaspoon coarse Kosher salt (1/4 teaspoon table salt)
Freshly ground black pepper to taste

"Tis better to have loved and lost
Than never to have loved at all."
Alfred Lord Tennyson

Ecstasy Entrees

"There is no love sincerer than the love of food."

George Bernard Shaw

Meat Melodies	Femme Fatale Meat Loaf with Flirty Red Peppers and Sex Kitten Onions
	Luscious London Broil with Bootilicious Cherry-Balsamic infusion
Games of Love or Lust	Lady Luck Duck with Cherry Infusion
	Maple Roasted Phuck Duck with Rosemary, Thyme, and Garlic Infusion
Fish Fantasy	Tempestuous Tilapia with Chile Infusion and Steamy Asparagus
	Sultry and Slinky Red Snapper with Ginger-Garlic-Sesame Infusion and Scallions
Poultry Obsession	Crush-Crazy Chicken with Amour Artichokes and Sultry Sundried Tomatoes
	Horny-Honey Chicken with Pineapple, Curry, and Dijon Mustard infusion
Pasta Infatuation	Tantilizing Pasta and Sexed Up Tomato Sauce with Anchovies, Olives, and Capers
	Naughty Noodles and Lusty Chicken with Peanut-Chile-Garlic Infusion and Vegetable Medley
Vegetarian Mania and Martyrdom	Love Drunk Lentil Almond Burgers with an Infusion of Carrots, Celery, and Shallots
	Sweetheart Eggplant Lasagna with an Infusion of Mushrooms, Mozzarella, and Zucchini

Meat Melodies of Steamy Lust and Conquest

Femme Fatale Meat Loaf
with Flirty Red Peppers and Sex Kitten Onions

Main Ingredients:
2 pounds lean ground beef
1 diced red pepper (about 1 cup)
1/2 diced yellow onion (about 3/4 cup)
2 large eggs, lightly beaten

Spices:
1 clove garlic, minced
1 bay leaf
2 tablespoons chopped fresh flat-leaf parsley
2 teaspoons chopped fresh thyme

Seasonings:
1 tablespoon olive oil
3/4 cup dry breadcrumbs
1 cup ketchup
1 tablespoon Worcestershire sauce
2 teaspoons kosher salt
1 teaspoon freshly ground black pepper

Cooking Instructions
Prepare the Vegetables:
1. Heat the olive oil in a skillet
2. Sauté the onions, garlic, and bay leaf until the onions are tender (3 minutes)
3. Add the diced red peppers and cook until the red peppers are tender (5 minutes)
4. Stir in the parsley and thyme and cook (2 minutes); then remove from heat and cool

Prepare the Meatloaf:
1. Preheat the oven to 350°
2. Line a baking sheet with parchment paper and spray lightly with oil
3. In a large bowl, combine the beef, eggs, bread crumbs, 1/2 cup of ketchup, Worcestershire sauce, salt, pepper, and sautéd vegetables
4. Transfer the mixture to a baking sheet and form into a loaf
5. Coat the meat loaf with the remaining 1/2 cup ketchup
6. Bake for 1-1 1/2 hours
7. Let set for about 5 minutes before slicing

Transfer Femme Fatale Meat Loaf to plate, serve with a side dish, and devour

Meat Melodies of Steamy Lust and Conquest

Luscious London Broil
with Bootilicious Cherry-Balsamic infusion

Main Ingredients:
1 1/2 pounds London broil, trimmed
3 tablespoons finely chopped shallot
2 tablespoons cherry preserves

Spices:
2 cloves garlic, minced

Seasonings:
1/2 cup dry red wine
1/4 cup balsamic vinegar
1/2 teaspoon salt
Freshly ground pepper to taste
1 teaspoon extra-virgin olive oil
2 teaspoons butter

Cooking Instructions
Prepare Cherry-Balsalmic Marinade:
1. Mix wine, vinegar, cherry preserves, garlic, salt and pepper in a small bowl

Prepare to Marinate London Broil:
1. Place meat in a shallow glass dish
2. Pour the marinade over the meat and turn to coat
3. Cover and marinate in the refrigerator, turning several times
4. Marinate the meat for up to 8 hours
5. Bring the marinade to a boil and reduce to a 1/2 cup
6. Remove from the heat, add butter, and whisk until melted

Prepare to Cook London Broil (Skillet, Broiler or Grill):
1. Brush a skillet with oil and heat over medium-high heat
2. Add the meat and cook for 10 to 12 minutes per side (meat forms a crust)
3. Transfer the meat to a cutting board (rest for 5 minutes)
4. Slice the meat thinly against the grain
5. Top with cherry-basalmic marinade
   Transfer Luscious London Broil to plate, serve with side dish, and devour

Poultry Ardor and Obsession

Crush-Crazy Chicken
with Amour Artichokes, and Sultry Sundried Tomatoes

Main Ingredients:
4 whole boneless chicken breasts
2 cups artichoke hearts, quartered (15 oz. can)
1/4 cup sundried tomatoes, julienne cut, soaked in hot water for 5 minutes, drained
1 small onion, diced
1/4 cup toasted pinenuts
1 cup white wine or chicken broth

Spices:
2 cloves garlic, minced
1/4 cup chopped fresh parsley

Seasonings:
1/2 cup all purpose flour seasoned with salt and pepper
2 tablespoons of olive oil
salt and pepper to taste

Cooking Instructions
Prepare Chicken:
1. Place chicken breasts in flour, toss well
2. Heat olive oil in large skillet
3. Add onion and garlic; saute 1 minute
4. Add chicken pieces, shaking off excess flour
5. Saute until browned on all sides

Prepare Artichokes and Sundried Tomatoes:
1. Add the sundried tomatoes, artichokes, wine or broth, stir well
2. Cover, lower heat to simmer, cook 10 minutes or until thickened, and chicken is cooked through
3. Taste for seasoning
4. Place in serving bowl, top with chopped parsley, and toasted pinenuts

Transfer Crush-Crazy Chicken to plate, serve with a side dish, and devour

Poultry Ardor and Obsession

Horny-Honey Chicken
with Pineapple, Curry, and Dijon Mustard infusion

Main Ingredients:
4 whole boneless chicken breasts
1/2 cup honey
1/4 cup pineapple juice

Spices:
1 tablespoon Dijon mustard
1 teaspoon curry powder

Seasonings:
4 tablespoons butter
1 teaspoon salt

Cooking Instructions

Prepare Pineapple-Curry, Mustard Infusion:
1. Combine honey, pineapple juice, mustard, salt, and curry powder
2. Pour over chicken in a large bowl, coating well

Prepare Baked Chicken:
1. In a 9x13x2-inch baking dish, melt butter
2. Arrange chicken in baking dish
3. Bake, uncovered, about 1 hour at 375°
4. Turn chicken pieces over at least once during baking

Transfer Horny-Honey Chicken to plate, serve with a side dish, and devour

Games of Lust or Love

Lady Luck Cherry Duck
with Vegetable Medley of Carrots, Potatoes, and Turnips

Main Ingredients:
1 whole Muscovy duck (4 to 5 pounds)
Duck neck and giblets (optional; leave out liver
2 large Yukon gold potatoes, peeled, and cut into large chunks
2 carrots, peeled and cut into ½ inch rounds
1 large onion, quartered
1 large turnip, peeled and quartered
1 large sweet potato, peeled and cut into large chunks
3 cups fresh Bing cherries, pitted
8 star anise

Spices:
Pinch of ground cloves
1 teaspoon of cinnamon
6 sprigs thyme
2 bay leaves
3 cinnamon sticks
2 bulbs garlic, separated into cloves

Seasoning:
Kosher salt and freshly ground pepper
6 tablespoon of extra-virgin olive oil
3 cups red wine
1/4 cup sugar

Cooking Instructions
Prepare Vegetables:
1. Grind 6 star anise; place in a small bowl and mix with ground cloves and cinnamon
2. In a roasting pan, add potatoes, carrots, onion, turnip, and sweet potato
3. Sprinkle with half of spice mixture, salt and pepper, and 3 tablespoons olive oil
4. Toss until uniformly seasoned and coated with oil

Prepare Duck:
1. Preheat oven to 350°
2. Rinse duck in cold water and pat dry
3. Season generously inside and out with salt and pepper
4. Rub all over with remaining spice mixture and olive oil
5. Place duck, breast side up, on top of vegetables in roasting pan
6. Add thyme, bay leaves, and 2 cinnamon sticks
7. Cover pan tightly with aluminum foil, and roast for 2 hours
8. After duck has cooked for 2 hours, remove foil and baste with pan juices
9. Add garlic, replace foil, and cook until meat starts pulling away from the bone (2¼ hours more)
10. Remove from oven and discard foil, brush duck with cherry-wine syrup
11. Increase temperature to 375°, and roast until skin gets crispy and dark brown (15 minutes)

Prepare Cherry Sauce:
1. In a saucepan, combine cherries, red wine, sugar, remaining whole star anise, and cinnamon stick
2. Cook over low heat until cherries are soft and wine has reduced to a syrup (30 minutes)
3. Transfer the rest to a small serving bowl for use as a compote
   Transfer Lady Luck Cherry Duck to plate and devour

Games of Lust or Love

Maple Roasted Love Duck
with Rosemary, Thyme and Garlic Infusion

Main Ingredients:
1 (3 1/2-pound) whole duck
1 small yellow onion, sliced in half

Spices:
1 head garlic, cloves separated and unpeeled
1 bunch fresh thyme
1 bunch fresh parsley
1 bunch fresh rosemary

Seasonings:
2 tablespoons kosher salt
1 tablespoon pepper
1/2 cup red wine vinegar
1 cup Vermont maple syrup

Cooking Instructions
Prepare Duck:
1. Remove innards from cavity of duck
2. Wash duck thoroughly
3. Preheat oven to 350°

Stuff Duck:
1. Fill duck with onion, garlic, thyme, rosemary, parsley, salt and pepper

Prepare Maple Glaze:
1. In a small bowl, combine vinegar and maple syrup
2. Brush outside of bird liberally with mixture

Cook Duck:
1. Place duck on roasting rack and cook 1 hour
2. Glazing periodically with maple glaze

Transfer Maple Roasted Love Duck to plate, serve with a side dish, and devour

Fish Fantasy and Fixation

Tempestuous Tilapia
with Chile Infusion and Steamy Asparagus

Main Ingredients:
1 pound Tilapia
2 pounds of asparagus

Spices:
2 tablespoons chile powder
1/2 teaspoon garlic

Seasonings:
1/2 teaspoon salt
2 tablespoons extra-virgin olive oil
3 tablespoons lemon juice

Cooking Instructions
Prepare Asparagus:
1. Bring 1 inch of water to a boil in a large saucepan
2. Put asparagus in a steamer basket, cover, until tender-crisp (4 minutes)

Prepare Tilapia:
1. Combine chile powder, garlic powder and 1/4 teaspoon salt on a plate
2. Dredge fillets in the spice mixture to coat
3. Heat oil in a large nonstick skillet over medium-high heat
4. Add the fish and cook until just opaque in the center (5 -7 minutes)
5. Add lemon juice, and remaining 1/4 teaspoon salt
6. Remove fish
7. Add asparagus to pan and coat with spices and seasonings (2 minutes)

Transfer Tempestuous Tilapia to plate, serve with a side dish, and devour

Fish Fantasy and Fixation

Sultry and Slinky Red Snapper
with Ginger-Garlic-Sesame Infusion and Scallions

Main Ingredients:
1 pound Red Snapper
(or Halibut or Bass: Any flaky white fish)

Spices:
6 1/4-inch-thick slices peeled fresh ginger
1/4 cup minced peeled fresh ginger
1/4 cup chopped garlic
1/4 cup sesame seeds
2-3 scallions, thinly sliced, for garnish

Seasonings:
2 tablespoons grapeseed oil or canola oil
2 tablespoons toasted sesame oil
1/4 cup reduced-sodium soy sauce

Cooking Instructions
Prepare Red Snapper:
1. Bring 1-2 inches of water to a boil in a large saucepan that can hold a steamer
2. Put a heatproof plate on the steamer
3. Place fish on plate with a slice of fresh ginger on top
4. Cover and steam over boiling water (5-7 minutes)

Prepare Ginger-Garlic-Sesame Infusion Sauce:
1. Combine minced ginger, garlic and sesame seeds in a small bowl
2. Heat grapeseed (or canola) oil in a medium skillet over medium-high heat
3. Add the ginger mixture and cook, stirring until fragrant (1 minute)
4. Add sesame oil (allow mixture to get hot)
5. Add soy sauce (careful, may splatter) and cook (1-2 minutes)
6. Transfer the fish to a deep platter
7. Discard the ginger slices
8. Pour the sauce over the fish
9. Garnish with scallions

Transfer Sultry and Slinky Red Snapper to plate, serve with a side dish, and devour

Pasta Infatuation or Addiction
Tantilizing Pasta and Sexed Up Tomato Sauce
with an Infusion of Anchovies, Olives, and Capers

Main Ingredients:
14 ounces spaghetti
2 tomatoes, chopped
2 tablespoons capers
4 tablespoons black olives, pitted
5 anchovy fillets, finely chopped

Seasoning:
2 tablespoons tomato passata
5 tablespoons extra-virgin olive oil, divided
Salt and pepper

Spice: Bunch of basil

Cooking Instructions
Prepare Pasta:
1. Put a large pot of water on to boil for cooking pasta
2. Cook pasta in the boiling water until not quite tender, about 1 minute less than specified in the package directions
3. When the pasta is cooked, drain, reserve the cooking water

Prepare Anchovies-Olives-Caper Infusion:
1. Combine capers, pitted black olives, finely chopped anchovy fillets, chopped tomatoes, and tomato passata, with 1/2 the olive oil, mix well (don't cook)
2. Steam the ingredients for the sauce over the top of the pasta pan, and let flavors infuse
3. Add the pasta to the sauce and toss well, adding some cooking water (if necessary)
4. Add the rest of the olive oil and toss again
5. Tear the basil leaves, scatter over the top and toss again

Transfer Tantilizing Pasta and Sexed Up Tomato Sauce to plate and devour

Pasta Infatuation or Addiction
Naughty Noodles and Lusty Chicken
with Peanut-Chile-Garlic Infusion and Vegetable Medley

Main Ingredients:
8 ounces whole-wheat spaghetti
1 pound boneless, skinless chicken breasts
1 12-ounce bag fresh vegetable medley, such as carrots, broccoli, and snow peas

Seasoning:
1/2 cup smooth natural peanut butter
2 tablespoons reduced-sodium soy sauce

Spices:
2 teaspoons minced garlic
1 1/2 teaspoons chile-garlic sauce
1 teaspoon minced fresh ginger

Cooking Instructions
Prepare Pasta and Vegetables:
1. Put a large pot of water on to boil for cooking pasta
2. Cook pasta in the boiling water until not quite tender, about 1 minute less than specified in the package directions
3. Add vegetables and cook until the pasta and vegetables are just tender (1-2 minutes)
4. Drain, reserving 1 cup of the cooking liquid and add to sauce (see below)

Prepare Chicken:
1. Place chicken in a skillet or saucepan and add enough water to cover; bring to a boil
2. Cover, reduce heat to low and simmer gently until cooked, no longer pink in the middle (10 to 12 minutes)
3. Transfer the chicken to a cutting board
4. When cool enough to handle, shred into bite-size strips

Prepare Peanut, Chile-Garlic Infusion Sauce:
1. Whisk peanut butter, soy sauce, garlic, chile-garlic sauce, and ginger in a large bowl
2. Stir in 1 cup of reserved cooking liquid from pasta and vegetables
3. Add the pasta, vegetables, and chicken; toss well to coat

Transfer Naughty Noodles and Lusty Chicken to plate, serve with a side dish, and devour

Vegetarian Mania and Martyrdom

Love Drunk Lentil Almond Burgers
with an Infusion of Carrots, Celery, and Shallots

Main Ingredients:
1 cup brown lentils or green French lentils
6 cups water
3/4 cup finely chopped carrot
1/3 cup finely chopped shallots (about 2 medium)
1/3 cup finely chopped celery (about 1 stalk)
1/4 cup sliced almonds

Spices:
1 teaspoon chopped fresh thyme

Seasonings:
2 tablespoons extra-virgin olive oil
1/2 teaspoon salt
1/4 teaspoon freshly ground pepper
1 large egg yolk, lightly beaten
1 tablespoon lemon juice

Cooking Instructions
Prepare Lentils:
1. Bring water to a boil in a large saucepan
2. Stir in lentils, reduce heat to medium-low, and simmer (25-30 minutes)
3. Drain in a fine-mesh sieve

Prepare Vegetables, Then Add Lentils:
1. Heat 1 tablespoon oil in a large skillet over medium heat
2. Add carrot, shallots, celery, and cook, stirring, until softened (3 minutes)
3. Add almonds, thyme, salt and pepper; continue cooking until the almonds are lightly browned (2 minutes)
4. Transfer the mixture to a food processor; add 1 cup of the cooked lentils (pulse several times, until the mixture is coarsely ground)
5. Transfer to a large bowl; stir in the remaining lentils, let cool for 10 minutes
6. Mix in egg yolk and lemon juice
7. Cover and refrigerate for 1 hour
8. Form the lentil mixture into 5 patties
9. Heat 1 tablespoon oil, add the patties and cook (3 to 4 minutes)
10. Turn gently and continue to cook until lightly browned (3 to 4 minutes)

Transfer Love Drunk Lentil Almond Burgers to plate and devour

Vegetarian Mania and Martyrdom

Sweetheart Eggplant Lasagna
with an Infusion of Mushrooms, Mozzarella, and Zucchini

Main Ingredients:
1 pound box lasagna noodles

Cheese:
24 ounces low-fat cottage cheese (or ricotta cheese)
32 ounces shredded mozzarella cheese

Vegetables:
2 eggplants, cut into circular slices 1/4–1/8-inch thick
6 to 8 zucchini, cut lengthwise into slices 1/4–1/8-inch thick
5 to 6 portobello mushrooms, thinly sliced
2 red onions, thinly sliced, and 3/4 cup chopped onions
2 cans (28 ounces) diced tomatoes and 6 cups marinara sauce (store bought)

Spices:
1/2 cup chopped herbs
(basil, oregano, or thyme)
4 cloves garlic
1/3 cup chopped basil

Seasoning:
4 tablespoons olive oil

Cooking Instructions
Prepare the Vegetables:
1. Sauté or oven-roast the vegetables until they are cooked through, set aside

Prepare the Marinara:
1. Heat olive oil, add chopped onions, and then add garlic and tomatoes and simmer (25 minutes)
2. Stir in the basil, add salt, and pepper to taste, simmer (10 minutes)

Prepare the Lasagna:
1. Preheat the oven to 350°
2. In the bottom of a 16" x 12" disposable pan, place a layer of dry noodles
3. On top of that, add about 1/3 of the marinara sauce, about 1/2 of the cottage cheese, and about 1/3 of the mozzarella cheese
4. Sprinkle herbs over the top, and add a layer of vegetables
5. Repeat the process (steps 2-4)
6. Finish with a layer of noodles, top with tomato sauce, and a thick layer of mozzarella cheese
7. Cover the pan with plastic wrap, then wrap tightly with aluminum foil
8. Bake for 35 minutes (until a knife pokes easily through the lasagna)
9. Remove the plastic and foil and bake at 450° (10 minutes) or until the top is browned
10. Remove lasagna from the oven and let sit (20 minutes)
11. Garnish with fresh basil leaves

THAT KISS

Fortune teller that I AM,
My crystal ball sees ALL.
Clairvoyant, the man's libido is flamBOYant.
I SEE: ANIMAL MAGNETISM.
Inside of THAT KISS will be bliss.

Taking chances with amorous glances
He advances... Lips pouting-tongue tied:
THAT KISS: smOOch; smOOch.
When he romances: his gait prances,
his penis lances, his generosity enhances.
VOODOO, or DOO-YOU want dinner, dear?"
His heart dances....

Magician that he is
He has a loaded deck of cards
And wants to be my bodyguard.
Enchantment: a bag of mesmerizing tricks,
An ACE up his sleeve, a KING or a JACK
Are inside of his top hat of black.
Sleight of hand, THAT KISS is grand.

Wizardry: Pressed into his bosom
I am caught in his embraces, arms
Flailing, like a net above my head
His pounding heart is beating red.
THAT KISS tells ALL or just enough
to keep me Interested in ALL of his stuff.

Lips full of feelings, THAT KISS
Soft as rose petals, free of prickly thorns.
In the dark recesses of his mouth
I find my way by the light in his eyes
His smile is real, there is no disguise.

Even though we just met
I am caught in the tangled web of
A hot-blooded, Israeli-Englishman:
"A Jack of All of Love's Trades."
A rare mixed-breed, a British accent,
Concealing a *Sabra, wherever he went.
Tricks of my own trade, I roll up my sleeve,
And I become a woman-in-need(?)
THAT KISS I can't forget, and with no regret:
It is almost 4 a.m., and inside of my gypsy's
tent: Sm(OO)ch, sm(OO)ch
We are still one silhouette.

Animal Magetism:
Sm(OO)ch, sm(OO)ch,
Some call it v(OO)d(OO),
Most think it witchcraft,
Experts refer to it as "osculation."
Others call THAT KISS Kabbalah;
A kind of Jewish mysticism:
Many are in need of exorcism.

Sharon Esther Lampert
©WorldFamousPoems.com
©SharonEstherLampert.com
Book: "Sweet Nothings: Love Poetry"

Erotic Side Dishes

"I have made a lot of mistakes falling in love, and regretted most of them, but never the potatoes that went with them."
Nora Ephron, Heartburn

Hunk of Burning Love Sweet Potatoes
with Honey, Rosemary, and Chile Infusion

Main Ingredients:
2 1/2 pounds red-skinned sweet potatoes (yams)
1/4 cup, 2 green onions, thinly sliced diagonally
1 tablespoon minced shallot

Spices:
1 tablespoon chopped fresh rosemary
2 teaspoons Dijon mustard
1/4 cup chopped fresh Italian parsley
2 fresh chiles, seeded, diced

Seasonings:
Dash of Worcestershire sauce
1/4 cup olive oil
Canola oil or vegetable oil (for brushing)
1 1/2 tablespoons white wine vinegar
2 tablespoons honey

Prepare the Potatoes:
1. Cook sweet potatoes in large saucepan of boiling salted water (6 minutes)
2. Drain and add cold water to cool; then cover and chill for 1 hour
3. Peel and quarter lengthwise
4. Brush potato wedges with canola oil
5. Sprinkle with salt and pepper
6. Grill potatoes (2 minutes per side)

Prepare the Dressing:
1. Mix six ingredients in small bowl: Honey, white wine vinegar, rosemary, minced shallot, Dijon mustard, and Dash of Worcestershire sauce
2. Gradually whisk in olive oil
3. Season to taste with salt and pepper
4. Place potatoes, chiles, green onions, and parsley in large bowl
5. Drizzle dressing over; toss to coat
6. Season to taste with salt and pepper

Erotic Side Dishes

Orgasmic Corn
with Climactic Red, Green, and Yellow Peppers

Main Ingredients:
9 large ears of corn, each broken in half
3 red bell peppers
3 yellow bell peppers
3 green peppers

Spices:
3/4 cup plus 2 tablespoons finely chopped fresh basil

Seasonings:
Olive oil (for brushing)
1/4 cup (1/2 stick) unsalted butter

Prepare the Peppers:
1. Grill peppers until charred on all sides
2. Transfer to paper bag and roll top to close tightly and steam (10 minutes)
3. Peel and seed peppers
4. Cut into 1/2-inch-thick strips
5. Melt butter in heavy large skillet over medium-high heat and saute, add bell pepper strips (3-5 minutes)
6. Stir in 3/4 cup basil
7. Season to taste with salt and pepper

Prepare the Corn:
1. Brush corn with olive oil
2. Sprinkle with salt and pepper
3. Grill until charred in spots, turning occasionally (10 minutes)

Erotic Side Dishes

Titillating Orecchiette
With Roasted Broccoli, Walnuts, and Parmesan

Main Ingredients:
12 ounces orecchiette or some other short pasta (3 cups)
1 bunch broccoli (1 1/2 pounds), cut into small florets
1/2 cup walnuts, roughly chopped
1/4 cup grated Parmesan (1 ounce)

Spices:
2 cloves garlic, chopped

Seasonings:
1/4 cup olive oil
kosher salt and black pepper
2 tablespoons unsalted butter

Cooking Instructions
Prepare the Orecchiette:
1. Cook the pasta according to the package directions
2. Drain the pasta and return it to the pot
3. Reserve 3/4 cup of the cooking water

Prepare to Roast the Broccoli:
1. Mix together the broccoli, walnuts, oil, garlic, 1/2 teaspoon salt, and 1/4 teaspoon pepper
2. Place into an oven and roast, tossing once, until the broccoli is tender (18 to 20 minutes)

Final Steps:
1. Toss the pasta with the broccoli mixture, butter, and 1/2 cup of the reserved pasta water (step 3)
2. If the pasta appears dry, add more water
3. Sprinkle with the Parmesan chesse before serving

Erotic Side Dishes

Mata Hari Barley Risotto with Asparagus and Parmesan

Main Ingredients:
1 1/2 cups barley
1 pound asparagus, cut diagonally into 1-inch pieces
1/2 cup (2 ounces) grated Parmesan
1 cup dry white wine (such as Sauvignon Blanc)

Spices:
1 large yellow onion, finely chopped
1 large clove garlic, finely chopped

Seasonings:
5 cups low-sodium vegetable or chicken broth
2 tablespoons olive oil
1/2 teaspoon kosher salt
1/4 teaspoon black pepper

Cooking Instructions
Prepare the Risotto:

1. Heat oil in a large saucepan (over medium heat)

2. Add the onion and cook, stirring occasionally (7 minutes)

3. Add the garlic and cook (1 minute)

4. Add the barley and cook (2 minutes)

5. Stir in the wine and cook until the liquid is absorbed (3 minutes)

6. Warm the broth in a small saucepan over low heat, then add to barley

7. Add the asparagus with the last 1/2 cup of broth and cook until tender (30-35 minutes)

8. Remove from heat, season with the salt and pepper

9. Stir in the Parmesan

(* Mata Hari was an exotic dancer and courtesan who was executed by a firing squad for espionage during World War I)

"Cooking is like love.
It should be entered into with abandon or not at all."
Harriet Van Horne

"You Don't Find LOVE, You Create LOVE"
Sharon Esther Lampert
Poet, Philosopher, Prophet, Peacemaker, Prodigy

Desserts of Seduction

To Die For Chocolate Almond Torte and a Rainbow of Sun-Kissed Berries

Ingredients:
1/2 cup unsalted butter
8 ounces bittersweet chocolate, imported from Belgian
5 large eggs, separate out yolks
3/4 cup sugar
1 cup ground almonds
Confectioner's sugar

Berries: Raspberries, blueberries, strawberries, and blackberries

Baking Instructions:
1. Preheat oven to 375°
2. Line the bottom and side of a greased 9-inch springform pan with aluminum foil
3. Melt the butter or margarine with the chocolate in the top of a double boiler, then cool
4. Beat the egg yolks and the sugar till they become pale yellow
5. Mix the cooled butter and chocolate with the sugar and yolks
6. Add the nuts
7. Beat the egg whites till they are stiff, but not dry
8. Fold into the chocolate mixture
9. Place a pan of water on the bottom shelf of preheated oven to make the torte moister
10. Pour in the filling
11. Bake for 45 to 50 minutes
12. Remove from the oven and let rest on the counter (5 minutes)
13. Unmold and carefully peel off the foil and place on a plate upside down
14. Sprinkle with Confectioner's sugar

Plate, serve with berries and whipped cream, and devour

NO, I DON'T COOK

A MAN HAS NEVER COME TO MY HOME EXPECTING ME TO COOK DINNER; EVERY MAN WHO COMES TO MY HOME EXPECTS TO HAVE ME FOR DINNER

SHARON ESTHER LAMPERT
POET, PHILOSOPHER, PROPHET, PEACEMAKER, PRODIGY

©BOOK: "MY SHORT FUNNIES ON MY LONG FEELINGS"

Desserts of Seduction

Princess Kadimah's Ethereal Brownies
8TH Prophetess of Israel

Main Ingredients:
1 ½ cups flour
4 large eggs
1 cup unsweetened cocoa powder
½ cup chopped walnuts

Kitchen Cabinet Ingredients:
2 teaspoons of vanilla extract
2 cups sugar
1 cup untsalted butter, melted

Baking Instructions:
1. Preheat oven to 375 °
2. Grease and flour a 9-by-13-inch baking pan
3. In a large bowl, combine the sugar, cocoa powder, and butter
4. Add the eggs, one at a time, stirring only until blended
5. Add the flour, vanilla, and walnuts
6. Stir until all the ingredients are blended
7. Transfer the mixture into the pan
8. Bake for 20 to 25 minutes until the center is firm to the touch

Plate, serve with ice cream or sorbet, blueberry lemonade, and devour

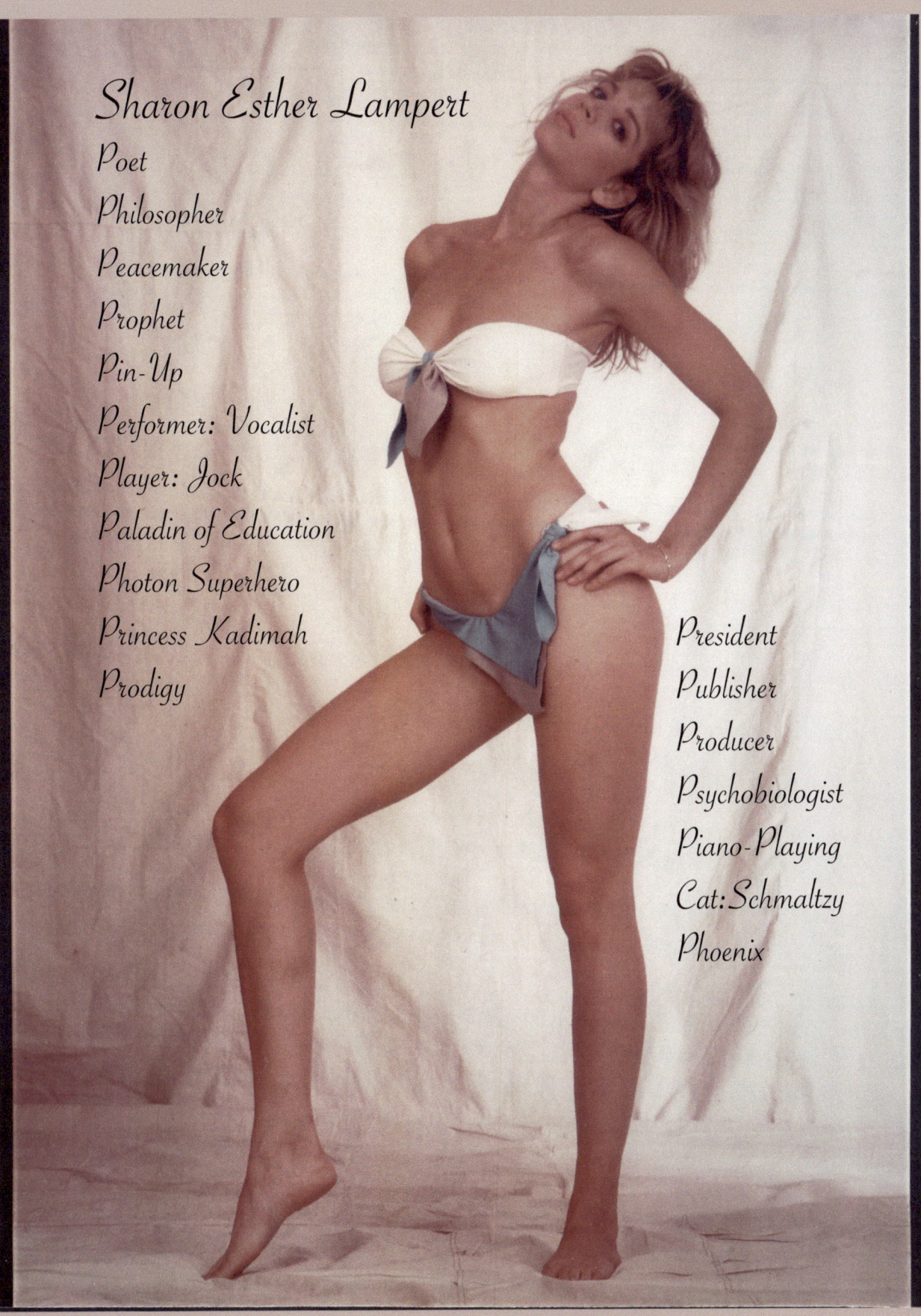

Desserts of Seduction

Dream Boat Creamy Obsession Cheesecake

Crust:
6 tablespoons unsalted butter
1 1/2 cups graham cracker crumbs
2 tablespoons sugar
Pinch fine salt

Filling:
2 pounds cream cheese at room temperature
2 cups sugar
1 cup sour cream
6 large eggs, lightly beaten
2 tablespoons vanilla paste or extract
1 teaspoon finely grated lemon zest
1 teaspoon finely grated orange zest

Prepare Crust:
1. Brush a 9-inch springform pan with some of melted butter
2. Stir the remaining butter together with the crumbs, sugar, and salt
3. Press the crumb mixture over the bottom of the pan
4. Bake until golden brown (15 to 18 minutes), then cool
5. Wrap the bottom and sides of the pan with foil and put it in a roasting pan

Prepare Cheesecake:
1. Filling: Beat the cream cheese until smooth
2. Add 1 1/4 cups sugar and beat just until light and fluffy
3. Slowly beat in 3/4 cup sour cream, then eggs, 1 tablespoon vanilla and both citrus zests
4. Pour into the cooled crust
5. Bring a medium saucepan or kettle of water to a boil
6. Gently place the roasting pan in the oven
7. Pour in enough hot water to come about halfway up the side of the pan
8. Bake the cheesecake (1 hour and 10 minutes)

Prepare Sourcream Topping:
1. Stir together the remaining sour cream, sugar, and vanilla paste
2. Spread over the top of the cooked cheesecake and return to the oven (for 5 minutes)
3. Turn the oven off, cook the cheesecake in the residual heat in the oven (for 1 hour)
4. Run a knife around the edges and cool to room temperature
5. Cover and refrigerate (at least 8 hours or overnight)

Love Conquers All: Midnight Intercourses

"When I find a man who makes love to me eight times on the 8th night of Hanukkah, I'll marry him!"
Sharon Esther Lampert

Sex Kitten Chocolate-Dipped Strawberries

Lovemaking requires stamina, and fresh fruit covered with chocolate is the high-octane fuel required to keep your lover in top form. You can use citrus fruits or berries, such as, pineapples, cherries, oranges, pears, or strawberries. Don't serve caffeinated drinks because sleep is required after lovemaking sessions. Refreshing lemonade is the best option and can be mixed with fruit, e.g., pink lemonade, blueberry lemonade, or watermelon lemonade.

Ingredients:
25 large strawberries
1 (12 ounce) bag dark chocolate chips, imported from Belgian
1 tablespoon vegetable oil

Cooking Instructions:
1. Clean and dry strawberries, leaving stems and leaves intact

2. In double boiler, over low heat, melt chocolate and oil, stir to combine

3. When using white chocolate chips, more oil may be needed to achieve a drizzling consistency

4. Lay wax paper on flat surface

5. Dip strawberries one by one into chocolate mixture, allowing extra chocolate to drip off

6. Place on wax paper to set

7. Refrigerate to set chocolate (10 minutes)

Love Conquers All: Midnight Intercourse

Sex Bomb Chocolate-Dipped Marshmallows

Ingredients:
12 marshmallows
2 ounces semisweet chocolate, melted
1 tablespoon vegetable oil

The Toppings:
Mixture of nuts
Nuts and shredded coconut
Blueberries and raspberries
Chopped pistachios and crumbled graham crackers

Cooking Instructions:
1. In double boiler, over low heat, melt chocolate and oil; stir to combine

2. Lay wax paper on flat surface

3. Dip half of each marshmallow into the melted chocolate, letting the excess drip off, then sprinkle with your desired toppings

4. Place on wax paper to set

5. Refrigerate to set chocolate (5-10 minutes)

- Serve with refreshing pink lemonade and devour
- Use your fingers to feed your lover by inserting the special treat directly into the mouth

Love Conquers All: Midnight Intercourses

Libido Lemonade to Maintain Sexual Stamina

Lemonade
3/4 cup sugar (if you use ultra-fine sugar, you don't have to heat sugar and water)
1 cup water
1 cup lemon juice (4 to 6 lemons = one cup of juice)
3 to 4 cups cold water (to dilute)

Cooking Instructions: (Serves 6)
1. Heat the sugar and water in a small saucepan until sugar is dissolved
2. Add the lemon juice and sugar water to a pitcher
3. Add 3 to 4 cups of cold water
4. Refrigerate 30 to 40 minutes
5. If the lemonade is too sweet for your taste, add lemon juice to it
6. Serve with ice and sliced lemons

Pink Lemonade:
Add 1 cup of unsweetened cranberry juice to lemonade

Watermelon Lemonade:
Liquify 2 cups of watermelon in a blender and add to lemonade

Blueberry Lemonade:
Liquify 2 cups of blueberries in a blender and add to lemonade

Strawberry Lemonade:
Liquify 2 cups of strawberries in a blender and add to lemonade

Raspberry Lemonade:
Liquify 2 cups of raspberrries in a blender and add to lemonade

Lavender Lemonade:
Place 1/4 cup dried lavender into a bowl, and pour boiling water over it; allow to steep for about 10 minutes, then strain out the lavender and discard; add to lemonade

Sharon Esther Lampert
Poet
Philosopher
Peacemaker
Prophet
Paladin of Education
Photon Superhero
Pin-Up
Performer; Vocalist
Player: Jock
Princess Kadimah
President
Publisher
Psychobiologist
Piano-Playing Cat
Phoenix

Food As Foreplay: Erogenous Zones

"Sex is Emotion in Motion"

Mae West

Erogenous zones are areas on the body with a dense number of nerve endings. If these nerve endings become stimulated, they elicit a sexual response and pleasurable feelings. The three major erogenous zones are the mind, heart, and body. Here are eighteen ways to touch and set a loved one on fire for a night of sexual ecstasy.

Erogenous Zone 1 : Your Lover's Mind
1. 85% of communication is non-verbal; pay attention to body language
2. First impressions last a lifetime
3. Make eye contact and smile
4. Dress appropriately; pay attention to your appearance
5. Ladies first, allow her to go first through doors and corridors
6. Men lead the way if you're about to go through a crowd

Erogenous Zone 2: Your Lover's Heart
7. Give something of yourself before you ask for something for yourself
8. Be generous with compliments; always have something loving to say
9. Never arrive empty-handed; always bring a token of affection for a loved one

Erogenous Zone 3: Your Lover's Body
10. Put your arm around a shoulder or waist, or hold a hand
11. Touch the back of the neck and the small of the back
12. Partner dancing, such as salsa, tango, or swing, can be a good way to break the touch barrier
13. Nibble the earlobes and explore behind the ears with your tongue softly
14. Do everything slowly from undressing, hugging, and caressing
15. The lower lips are sucked and bitten
16. Nipples differ in sensitivity and some may like it to be stroked, sucked, and licked
17. Hot zones for men: Male sexual organ, scrotum, rigged area of skin between testicles and anus and buttocks
18. Hot zone for women: The orgasmic erogenous zone of a woman is the clitoris; the skin over the clitoris is packed with nerve endings and becomes rigid if massaged with the finger or tongue

"All happiness depends upon a leisurely breakfast."
John Gunther

LUVU

LOVE, UNDERSTAND, VALIDATE, UNCONDITIONAL

A Romantic Kissy Brunch

Love Drenched Challah French Toast
with Slivers of Sliced Bananas, Blueberries, Strawberries, and a Slice of Orange

Main Ingredients:
1 large loaf challah or brioche bread
6 extra-large eggs
1 1/2 cups half-and-half or milk
1 teaspoon grated orange zest

Seasoning:
1/2 teaspoon pure vanilla extract
1 tablespoon honey
1/2 teaspoon kosher salt
Unsalted butter
Vegetable oil

Cooking Instructions:
1. Preheat the oven to 250^0

2. Whisk together the eggs, half-and-half, orange zest, vanilla, honey, and salt

3. Slice the challah in 3/4-inch thick slices

4. Soak the slices in the egg mixture, turning once

5. Heat 1 tablespoon butter and 1 tablespoon oil in a saute pan over medium heat

6. Add the soaked bread and cook on each side, until nicely browned (2-3 minutes)

7. Serve hot with maple syrup and sprinkle lightly with Confectioner's sugar

8. Add a sliced banana, a handful of blueberries, three strawberries, and a slice of orange to the plate

Plate, serve, and devour

A Romantic Kissy Brunch
Voluptuous Lemon Buttermilk Blueberry Pancakes

Main Ingredients:
1 1/2 cups unbleached all-purpose flour
1 1/3 cups buttermilk
2 large eggs, separated
2 cups fresh blueberries
lemon zest
1 stick cinnamon

Kitchen Cabinet Ingredients:
3 tablespoons cane sugar
1 teaspoon baking powder
1/2 teaspoon baking soda
1/2 teaspoon salt
2 tablespoons vegetable oil
1 tablespoon plus 1 teaspoon of lemon zest
1/8 teaspoon vanilla extract
Pinch cream of tartar
Butter for pan

Cooking Instructions:
1. Mix (dry) together: Flour, sugar, baking powder, baking soda and salt, set aside
2. Mix (wet) together: Egg yolks, oil, buttermilk, lemon zest and vanilla extract
3. Make a well in the center of the dry ingredients and pour in the liquid mixture
4. In a small bowl, beat egg whites, and cream of tartar until soft peaks form
5. Fold the egg whites into the batter just until incorporated
6. Let set for 15 minutes and gently fold in the blueberries
7. Heat a nonstick pan or cast iron griddle over medium heat
8. Brush with the butter and heat until the butter just begins to sizzle
9. Pour 1/4 cup batter into pan and cook until golden brown (1 to 1 1/2 minutes)
10. Flip over and cook until the bottom is lightly golden brown, about 45 seconds

Blueberry Syrup for Pancakes
Ingredients:
1/2 cup maple syrup, 1 1/2 cups blueberries, 2 tablespoons sugar, 1 stick cinnamon, lemon zest

Cooking Instructions:
1. Mix together the maple syrup, blueberries, sugar, cinnamon stick, and lemon zest and bring to a boil, then simmer over low heat (15 minutes)
2. Pour into a jug and bring to the breakfast table with the pancakes

A Romantic Kissy Brunch
Addicted to Love and Cheese Blintzes

Ingredients:
1 cup flour
1 package vanilla sugar
Pinch of salt
1/4 cup sugar
4 eggs
1/2 cup milk
1/2 cup water
1 tablespoon of oil

Cheese Filling I
1/2 pound farmer cheese
4 ounces cream cheese
4 tablespoons of honey or maple syrup
juice of 1/2 lemon
1 egg yolk

Cheese Filling II
1 pound cottage cheese, strained
2 egg yolks
2 tablespoons of flour
2 tablespoons of sugar
1 teaspoon of vanilla sugar
1/4 cup raisins (optional)

Cooking Instructions
Prepare the Dough:
1. In a large mixer bowl combine eggs, milk, and water, blend well
2. Gradually add flour, then both sugars, salt and oil
3. Beat well until there are no lumps in the batter
4. Ladle approximately 1/3 cup of batter into the skillet
5. Fry on one side until until golden brown

Prepare the Filling:
1. Combine all ingredients in a bowl and beat well or in a blender until smooth

Fill the Blinzes:
1. Add 3 tablespoons of filling on one edge in a 2 1/2 inch long by 1-inch wide mound
2. Roll once to cover filling
3. Fold the sides into the center and continue rolling until completely closed
4. Heat 2 tablespoons of oil in the skillet and place each crepe seam side down in the skillet and fry 2 minutes on each side, turning once

Plate, serve, and devour

A Goody Bag of Sweet Surrender

Casanova Chocolate Marshmallow Fudge

Send your lover home with a goody bag filled with sweet treats filled with fond memories of your time together. Your lover will have treats to last a week long until your get together. Of course, add a handwritten love note of sweet nothings addressed to his or her pet name.

Main Ingredients:
1 pint marshmallow cream
2 twelve-ounce packages chocolate chips
1 pound of nuts of choice
(almonds, walnuts, peanuts, pecans, hazelnuts)
1 twelve-ounce can evaporated milk

Kitchen Cabinet Ingredients:
4 cups sugar
1/2 cup plus 2 tablespoons unsalted butter
1 teaspoon vanilla

Cooking Directions:
1. Grease a 9×13 baking dish with 2 tablespoons of butter
2. In a medium saucepan over medium heat, combine sugar, remaining butter and evaporated milk
3. Stir and bring to a boil and cook until sugar evaporates (5-10 minutes)
4. Add chocolate chips and vanilla, mix until melted
5. Add marshmallow cream, blend well
6. Stir in nuts
7. Pour mixture into baking dish and allow to cool completely
8. Cut fudge into chunks
9. Store in airtight container

Wrap in a gift bag and send your lover off with a goody bag of sweets

A Goody Bag of Sweet Surrender

Salome Chocolate-Cognac-Almond Truffles

Main Ingredients:
8 ounces semisweet or bittersweet chocolate
3/4 cup heavy cream
2 tablespoons unsalted butter
2 tablespoons alcohol (cognac, brandy, Grand Marnier, rum, bourbon, or Kahlua)
slivered almonds

Choose a Topping
Different Coatings for Truffles:
a. cocoa powder
b. Confectioner's sugar (icing or powdered)
c. toasted and chopped nuts
   (pecans, walnuts, almonds, hazelnuts)
d. toasted coconut
e. shaved chocolate

Cooking Instructions
Part 1:
1. Chop chocolate into small pieces
2. Heat the cream and butter and bring to a boil
3. Pour the boiling cream over the chocolate, let stand for 5 minutes
4. Stir with a whisk until smooth, add the liqueur, add slivered almonds
5. Cover and place in the refrigerator until firm (several hours or overnight)

Part II:
6. Form the chocolate into round or mis-shaped bite-sized balls
7. Roll the truffle in the topping of choice and place on a parchment
8. Cover and place in the refrigerator until firm
9. Bring to room temperature before serving
10. Store in airtight container

Wrap in a gift bag and send your lover off with a goody bag of sweets

A Goody Bag of Sweet Surrender

Cleopatra Chocolate Hazelnut Biscotti

Main Ingredients:
1 3/4 cups all-purpose flour
4 ounces semisweet or bittersweet chocolate
For glaze: 3 ounces white chocolate
1/3 cup unsweetened cocoa
1 cup hazelnuts (toasted and chopped)
1 tablespoon instant espresso powder
3 large eggs

Kitchen Cabinet Ingredients:
1 cup firmly packed light brown sugar
1 teaspoon baking soda
1/4 teaspoon salt
1 1/2 teaspoons pure vanilla extract

Prepare the Nuts:
1. Preheat oven to 350,⁰, toast hazelnuts, spread on a baking sheet (15 minutes)
2. Place nuts in a dish towel and let nuts 'steam' for 5 minutes to remove the skins from the nuts, then cool and then chop coarsely

Prepare Biscotti:
1. In food processor, combine chopped chocolate and brown sugar, until very fine
2. Mix together the flour, cocoa, espresso powder, baking soda and salt in one bowl
3. Combine the eggs and vanilla extract and beat to blend in another bowl
4. Mix all together: The chocolate/sugar and flour mixtures until a stiff dough forms, then add the hazelnuts
5. On a floured surface divide the dough in half
6. Form each half into a log 12 inches long
7. Bake until almost firm to the touch (35 - 40 minutes)
8. White chocolate glaze: Melt 3 ounces of white chocolate over a saucepan of simmering water. Dip end of biscotti into chocolate, dry on parchment paper
9. Store in airtight container

Wrap in a gift bag and send your lover off with a goody bag of sweets

My Man
Making Love All Through the Night and All Through the Day

My Man is passionate and strong, all through
the night, I know his emotional,
spiritual, and physical being; I feel
the breadth and depth of his masculinity.

All through the night, My Man holds
me tightly in his arms: warm, tender,
and cuddly, childlike, always knowing
where I am, secure forevermore.

My Man's touch lingers,
I am sleeping soundly all
through the night, still making
love with him, in my dreams.

I awaken to My Man's soft kisses at
dawn, my spirit floating in the morning
mist, the promise of love is fulfilled,
my heart is murmuring a melody, a
sweet new song, all through the day.

Sharon Esther Lampert

© WorldFamousPoems.com
© SharonEstherLampert.com
Book: "Sweet Nothings: 40 Love Poems"

Conclusion: At Long Last, Love is Here to Stay

Ambrosia

In ancient Greek mythology, ambrosia is the food or the drink of the gods, and confers ageless immortality upon whoever consumes it. In modern times, ambrosia is packed with fiber, vitamins, and minerals and confers vigor and vitality, upon whoever consumes it.

Ingredients:
6 navel oranges
3 sliced bananas
1/2 pineapples cut into 1/2-inch cubes
1/2 cup shredded sweetened dried coconuts
1/2 cup miniature marshmallows
3 tablespoons of orange liqueur
Sprinkle ever so lightly Confectioner's sugar

Prepare Ambrosia:
1. Cut oranges into segments by cutting down against the membrane on either side (remove seeds)

2. Add the sliced bananas, pineapple cubes, and shredded coconut

3. Add the marshmallows

4. Add the orange liqueur

5. Sprinkle ever so lightly Confectioner's sugar

Plate, serve, and devour

Love ever Reborn Is Love ever Newborn
Sharon Esther Lampert

Driven by ever Delectable Delights of
Pure Perfections of Sweet-Skin Confections
Ever Enamoured
Sinewy Soft Skins Embrace
Ever Enkindled
Warm ever Tender Kisses ever Feverish Touching ever Retouching
Ever Entangled
Two Naked Souls are ever Woven as ever One
Ever Entwined
Ever Head To Head ever Heart To Heart ever Toe To Toe
Ever Engulfed
Caresses ever Consume ever Conquering evermore
Love ever Reborn Is Love ever Newborn

Ever Enveloped
Tightly Bound From Dusk Till Dawn Lovers Inextricably Embrace,
Ever Enveloped
Touchingly By Osmosis Powerful Emotions Permeate Satin Skins
Ever Enveloped
Ever Thrusting ever Churning to Mysterious Musical Muses
Ever Enveloped
Full Bodied Naked Souls Ferment in Infinite Emotional Depths
Ever Enveloped
Cloaked by Romantic Fantasies Desires Seductively Impel
Ever Enveloped
Thresholds of ever Towering Peaks of ever Tremendous Passions ever Arise
Ever Enveloped
Two Hearts Secure in an ever Sacred Union ever Harmonizing
Ever Enveloped
Ever Needing to be ever Accepted ever Cherished ever Unconditionally
Ever Enveloped
Two Together -- ever Feasting as One -- ever Body ever Mind ever Soul
Love ever Reborn Is Love ever Newborn

Ever Drawing Nearer . . . and ever Closer
Enticing, Ecstasy is ever Unabridged
Ever Drawing Nearer . . . and ever Closer
Enthalled, Ecstasy is ever Unbounded
Ever Drawing Nearer . . . and ever Closer
Enraptured, Ecstasy is ever Unbridled
Love ever Reborn Is Love ever Newborn

©WorldFamousPoems.com
"Sweet Nothings: Love Poems"

Ever Entwined in ever Endless Pretzels ever Unending
ever Intimacy ever Uninhibited,
ever Intimacy ever Unencumbered,
ever Intimacy ever Uncontaminated,
ever Hard, ever Longing for Physical
Recovery, ever Wanting to Begin Again,
ever Hard, Letting Go of His Body, His Warmth,
the Music of His Beating Heart, His Lips,
His Hands, the Blankets -- ever Unfurling
Love ever Reborn Is Love ever Newborn

Ever Ecstatic
Love is ever Reborn
In Yesterday's Daring Darkness of the Deepening Night
Ever Exalted
Love is ever Reborn
In-between the Slumber of One Sleepless Night and One Dreamy Day
Ever Exuberant
Love is ever Reborn
In Tomorrow's Penetrating Spiked Peaks of a Parting Sunrise
Love ever Reborn Is Love ever Newborn

Ever Effervescent
Lit By Catalytic Sunlight of the New Day
Lovers Separate
Ever Resolved and ever Unresolved
Ever Enriched
In ever Body ever Mind ever Soul
Love Rehomogenizes
Ever Resolved and ever Unresolved
Ever Enlightened
In a Love for the Self and a Love for the Other
Love Separates
Ever Resolved and ever Unresolved
Love ever Reborn Is Love ever Newborn

Ever Returning
An Enduring Hunger Remains
Ever Unforgettable
In Complete Recall
Ever Enshrined
In Eternally Memorable Time
Ever Endless
Love ever Never ever Ceasing
Ever Entrusted
Promising to Love All-Ways in ever Time ever Touch ever Intensity
Love ever Reborn Is Love ever Newborn

God Is a Woman

(1) Caressing my tender breasts,
his left hand's on the steering wheel,
and his right hand is firmly tucked
away inside my red silk dress.

(2) He swerves the car to the curb
and turns off the ignition. Filling his
hungry mouth with my tasty tongue
- both hands caress my breasts -
Dangling keys dance to the Israeli music
playing on the radio,"Chayal shel Ahavah."

(3) Too old to be making love
in the front seat of his red van,
on a hot summer's night,
street lights on, glaring,
headlights off, flaring,
the moonlight beaming,
or am I dreaming?

(4) Protruding, a bump below his
knee, a near-death experience:
the Israeli Army; inside Lebanon;
Sabra and Shatila; the fall; from
helicopter to hospital; an iron plate.
At home, fighting for his homeland,
a permanent dwelling; Iraqi parents
speaking Arabic, landed him on the
front lines of the bloody battlefield.
Jew, speak to your enemy in Arabic,
silently, with knives. A dangling gun
marches to military orders on the radio.

(5) Me: sipping a pink Cosmo at Cibar;
red brick exterior and red velvet interior.
Him: toasting a "L'Chaim" with a Strawberry
Daiquiri. He speaks to me, "Al-ha-ke-fak"
and he is teaching me; and I look at him and
I look inside him: an iron plate below his knee;
a locksmith for life;
a marriage gone sour;
an eviction after a lease expired;
an Orthodox Jew at a Chabad house;
his hands were full: battle, blood, and bump,
business and burden, bitch, Bible, and breast.

(6) Protruding, an engorged bump above
his knee, a near-life experience: an Israeli
man, an exotic accent, dark magnetic
eyes and chocolate-covered silk skin.
At home, in a temporary shelter, a sexy
exterior and a hot-blooded interior melted
me into his amorous arms. Melded together
as one, he speaks to his lover sweetly,
"Sing to me, Cha-mu-dah, of " Jerusalem of Gold," and of peace."

(7) Protrusions: An iron bump below his knee and
an engorged bump above his knee: a near-death
and a near-life experience: reaching again
for my ample breasts with loving hands and
a loving heart, suckling my pink nipples,
like a baby aching for his bottle of milk,
he speaks softly, whispering into his lover's ear,
"I love your breasts."
I ask, "How do you say breasts in Hebrew?"
"Shadayim, Mo-tek, shadayim."

8) Me: taking a spiritual detour, Shabbat at
the Chabad house, in a yellow dress that is
long enough to skim my knees, no protrusions,
only mystery. Illuminated is the fact that
in the Bible, the word Shaddai is God's name.
God speaks clearly with compassion:
God spoke to Moses and said to him:"I am Yahweh.
I appeared to Abraham, Isaac, and Jacob as El Shaddai."
Flickering Shabbat candles gleaming,
the moonlight beaming, or am I dreaming?
Shaddai provides a name of God that
celebrates the feminine attributes in God:
God Shaddai with shadayim-breasts.
Therefore, making perfect sense to me,
GOD IS A WOMAN. AL-HA-KE-FAK.

© WWW.WORLDFAMOUSPOEMS.COM

Sharon Esther Lampert

Remo: "Drink, Drink, Drink"

At Quattro Gatti, she is the poet-in-residence:
In Barcelona, Piccasso started here, painting
A humble sketch of a picket-white fence.

Tony: His speciality, a watermelon martini.
Filling her glass to the very brim,
He closes the doors, and the lights dim.

"Drink, drink, drink," He commands.

A dark Italian stallion, no doubt,
He pulls her bar stool closer to him,
Experienced in lust, he knows the route.

"Drink, drink, drink," He commands.

Before his eyes, he sees only a red flower,
And takes a whiff, along her long stemmed neck,
He breathes her scent in, and is ready to devour...

"Drink, drink, drink," He commands.

He longs for, and savors, a passionate kiss.
Skin soft like petals, and breasts ripe and firm
As rosebuds in bloom: it is after-working hours,
And he only has time to uproot the table flowers.

However, rumors abound: the waiters resound.
For an extra tip, they will spin a tale of love, quite profound:

Most say that he made love to her on top of his bar.
They say: She knocked over a glass, and still bears a scar.
Many agree that they made the bar their bed,
Leaving red lipstick stains painted in red.
Some say, they fell off their bar stools onto the floor
The neighbor next door says, he heard Tony roar.

Others say that they have the love story all wrong!
At Quattro Gatti, she is the poet-in-residence:
So making love to her on his bar,
Or taking her home in his car,
Is taking the romantic fantasy too far.

However, lingering in his air: a telltale sign.
He knows exactly where she is sitting,
Familiar with her perfumed scent, forevermore,
Whenever she enters his particular door.

The truth of their encounter, lives on in one of the four
Cats, sitting still on the window sill, wearing the bell:
One saw, one heard, one dreamt, and one played,
And loyal to their Master Tony, they will never tell.

Sharon Esther Lampert
© www.WorldFamousPoems.com

Sharon Esther Lampert
Poet
Philosopher
Prophet
Peacemaker
Paladin of Education
Photon Superhero
Pin-Up
Performer: Vocalist
Player: Jock
Princess Kadimah
Prodigy

Ani Ohev Otach [man to a woman]

Ani Ohevet Otcha [woman to a man]

Special Treat: Say "I Love You" in Forty Languages

1. Arabic
Ah'bika [to a man]
Ah'bik   [to a woman]

2. Cambodian
Bung Srorlagn Oun (to female)

3. Cantonese   Ngo oi ney
4. Chinese (Mandarin) Wo ai ni
5. Czech   Miluji tě
6. Danish   Jeg elsker dig
7. Dutch   Ik hou van jou
8. English   I love you
9. Finnish   Minä rakastan sinua
10. Flemish   Ik zie oe geerne
11. French   Je t'aime
12. German   Ich liebe Dich
13. Greek   S'agapo
14. Greenlandic   Asavakit
15. Hawaiian   Aloha wau ia oi

16. Hebrew
Ani ohevet otcha [woman to a man]
Ani ohev otach [man to a woman]
Ani ohev otcha [man to a man]
Ani ohevet otach [woman to a woman]

17. Hindi   Hum Tumhe Pyar Karte hae
18. Hungarian   Szeretlek te'ged
19. Icelandic   ég elska þig
20. Italian   Ti amo

21. Japanese   Ai shiteru
22. Korean   Tangsinul sarang ha yo
23. Lebanese   Bahibak
24. Moroccan   Ana moajaba bik
25. Navaho   Ayor anosh'ni
26. Nepali   Ma Timilai Maya Garchhu
27. Norwegian   Jeg elsker deg
28. Polish   Kocham Cie
29. Portuguese   Amo-te
30. Punjabi   Mai taunu pyar karda
31. Romanian   Te iubesc
32. Russian   Ya tyebya Lyublyu
33. Spanish   Te amo
34. Swedish   Jag älskar dig

35. Thai
Chan rak khun (to male)
Phom rak khun (to female)

36. Turkish   Seni seviyorum
37. Vietnamese   Aim ew ang [to a man]
38. Welsh   Rwy'n dy garu di
39. Yiddish   Ikh hob dikh lib
40. Zimbabwe   Ndinokuda

Song of Songs, Chapter 7, Love Poetry (Hebrew, p.133)

1. Return, return, O Shulammite; Return, return, that we may look upon thee. What will ye see in the Shulammite? As it were a dance of two companies.

2. How beautiful are thy steps in sandals, O prince's daughter! The roundings of thy thighs are like the links of a chain, the work of the hands of a skilled workman.

3. Thy navel is like a round goblet, wherein no mingled wine is wanting; thy belly is like a heap of wheat set about with lilies.

4. Thy two breasts are like two fawns that are twins of a gazelle.

5. Thy neck is as a tower of ivory; thine eyes as the pools in Heshbon, by the gate of Bath-rabbim; thy nose is like the tower of Lebanon which looketh toward Damascus.

6. Thy head upon thee is like Carmel, and the hair of thy head like purple; the king is held captive in the tresses thereof.

7. How fair and how pleasant art thou, O love, for delights!

8. This thy stature is like to a palm-tree, and thy breasts to clusters of grapes.

9. I said: 'I will climb up into the palm-tree, I will take hold of the branches thereof; and let thy breasts be as clusters of the vine, and the smell of thy countenance like apples;

10. And the roof of thy mouth like the best wine, that glideth down smoothly for my beloved, moving gently the lips of those that are asleep.

11. I am my beloved's, and his desire is toward me.

12. Come, my beloved, let us go forth into the field; let us lodge in the villages.

13. Let us get up early to the vineyards; let us see whether the vine hath budded, whether the vine-blossom be opened, and the pomegranates be in flower; there will I give thee my love.

14. The mandrakes give forth fragrance, and at our doors are all manner of precious fruits, new and old, which I have thee, O my beloved.

Song of Songs, Chapter 7, Read the Poem in Original Hebrew

א שׁוּבִי שׁוּבִי הַשּׁוּלַמִּית, שׁוּבִי שׁוּבִי וְנֶחֱזֶה-בָּךְ; מַה-תֶּחֱזוּ, בַּשּׁוּלַמִּית, כִּמְחֹלַת, הַמַּחֲנָיִם.

ב מַה-יָּפוּ פְעָמַיִךְ בַּנְּעָלִים, בַּת-נָדִיב; חַמּוּקֵי יְרֵכַיִךְ--כְּמוֹ חֲלָאִים, מַעֲשֵׂה יְדֵי אָמָּן.

ג שָׁרְרֵךְ אַגַּן הַסַּהַר, אַל-יֶחְסַר הַמָּזֶג; בִּטְנֵךְ עֲרֵמַת חִטִּים, סוּגָה בַּשּׁוֹשַׁנִּים.

ד שְׁנֵי שָׁדַיִךְ כִּשְׁנֵי עֳפָרִים, תָּאֳמֵי צְבִיָּה.

ה צַוָּארֵךְ, כְּמִגְדַּל הַשֵּׁן; עֵינַיִךְ בְּרֵכוֹת בְּחֶשְׁבּוֹן, עַל-שַׁעַר בַּת-רַבִּים--אַפֵּךְ כְּמִגְדַּל הַלְּבָנוֹן, צוֹפֶה פְּנֵי דַמָּשֶׂק.

ו רֹאשֵׁךְ עָלַיִךְ כַּכַּרְמֶל, וְדַלַּת רֹאשֵׁךְ כָּאַרְגָּמָן: מֶלֶךְ, אָסוּר בָּרְהָטִים.

ז מַה-יָּפִית, וּמַה-נָּעַמְתְּ--אַהֲבָה, בַּתַּעֲנוּגִים.

ח זֹאת קוֹמָתֵךְ דָּמְתָה לְתָמָר, וְשָׁדַיִךְ לְאַשְׁכֹּלוֹת.

ט אָמַרְתִּי אֶעֱלֶה בְתָמָר, אֹחֲזָה בְּסַנְסִנָּיו; וְיִהְיוּ-נָא שָׁדַיִךְ כְּאֶשְׁכְּלוֹת הַגֶּפֶן, וְרֵיחַ אַפֵּךְ כַּתַּפּוּחִים.

י וְחִכֵּךְ, כְּיֵין הַטּוֹב הוֹלֵךְ לְדוֹדִי לְמֵישָׁרִים; דּוֹבֵב, שִׂפְתֵי יְשֵׁנִים.

יא אֲנִי לְדוֹדִי, וְעָלַי תְּשׁוּקָתוֹ.

יב לְכָה דוֹדִי נֵצֵא הַשָּׂדֶה, נָלִינָה בַּכְּפָרִים.

יג נַשְׁכִּימָה, לַכְּרָמִים--נִרְאֶה אִם-פָּרְחָה הַגֶּפֶן פִּתַּח הַסְּמָדַר. הֵנֵצוּ הָרִמּוֹנִים: שָׁם אֶתֵּן אֶת-דֹּדַי. לָךְ.

יד הַדּוּדָאִים נָתְנוּ-רֵיחַ, וְעַל-פְּתָחֵינוּ כָּל-מְגָדִים--חֲדָשִׁים, גַּם-יְשָׁנִים; דּוֹדִי, צָפַנְתִּי לָךְ.

About the Author

V.E.S.S.E.L.
Very. Extra. Special. Sharon. Esther. Lampert.

Food is for the BODY
Education Is for the MIND and POETRY Is for the SOUL

MYLife Is an OPENBook To KNOWMe Is To READMe

www.PoetryJewels.com
Diamonds, Emeralds, Sapphires, Rubies, and Pearls

When I'm not writing, I'm reading.
When I'm not reading, I'm writing.
When I'm not writing or reading, I'm singing...

Sharon Esther Lampert

See The World Through The Eyes of a Creative

Sharon Esther Lampert
Gifted: Born with Extra-Body Part, a "Creative Apparatus"

POET
POETRY WORLD RECORD: 120 WORDS OF RHYME
GREATEST POEMS EVER WRITTEN ON EXTRAORDINARY WORLD EVENTS

PHILOSOPHER
GOD TALKS TO ME: A WORKING DEFINITION OF GOD
GOD OF WHAT? IS LIFE A GIFT OR A PUNISHMENT?
www.PhilosopherQueen.com

PROPHET
22 COMANDMENTS: ALL YOU WILL EVER NEED TO KNOW ABOUT GOD

PEACEMAKER
WORLD PEACE EQUATION

PALADIN OF EDUCATION
SMARTGRADES BRAIN POWER REVOLUTION
IN 24 HOURS, EARN A GRADES

40 UNIVERSAL GOLD STANDARDS OF EDUCATION

"THE SILENT CRISIS DESTROYING AMERICAS BRIGHTEST MINDS"
www.SMARTGRADES.com

PHOTON SUPERHERO
SUPERHERO OF EDUCATION
www.PhotonSuperHero.com

PRODIGY
10 ESOTERIC LAWS OF GENIUS AND CREATIVITY
40 RULES OF MANHOOD, www.SillyLittleBoys.com
GOD TALKS TO ME: A WORKING DEFINITION OF GOD
DOUBLE WHAMMY: A Working Definition of EVIL
10 MIRACLES: What Happens When You Free Your Mind of Negativity?

PRINCESS KADIMAH
8TH PROPHETESS OF ISRAEL

PIN-UP
SEXIEST CREATIVE GENIUS IN HUMAN HISTORY

The Sole Intention of My Poetry is to Add Light to Your Soul.
Sharon Esther Lampert

Letter from Mommy, Eve Lampert, to her Daughter, Sharon Esther, Age 9

Darling Sharon,

My Daughter is a Poet, Philosopher, and Teacher.

Beauty and Brains,

I Love You,

Mommy, XOXO

How to Read a Poem by Sharon Esther Lampert

1. Sharon's Poetry Paintings
Similar to the poet William Blake, her poems are accompanied by elaborate visual graphics that enrich and compliment the text. The poems are wall hangings, and her poems are framed by ardent fans and hang in their living spaces, like paintings.

2. Sharon is a Master of Condensation
Sharon is a master of the art of condensation. She is able to condense a major world event in world history into a one-page poem. Sharon can condense a 600-page book into a single page. Her immortal literary gems come in a variety of lengths: A single sentence, a single page, and grand sweeping epics.

3. Sharon is a Literary Photographer
Her poems are telescopic of the main event and microscopic of the infinite details.

4. Sharon Can Pack a Single Verse to the Brim
Sharon's poems are known for her ability to weave poetry, philosophy, and comedy into a single verse.

5. Documentary Poet: Poems are Cinematic Journey's Through History
Sharon's poems take you on a cinematic journey, and make you feel as if you are reliving the event, as if it happened today.

6. Sharon's Poems Are Completed Literary Works
Sharon's poems are completed works of art. Every word is essential to the poem. You cannot remove or replace a word. There are no extra words. Every word has its rightful place and fits to perfection.

7. Sharon's Poems Are All Inspired Works of Art
All of her poems are inspired. There are no rough drafts. Like giving birth to a baby, the poem incubates in her "creative apparatus," and is birthed in minutes. Like a baby, the poems are delivered whole and complete.

8. Sharon's Signature Endings: The Epiphany (Spiritual Illumination)
The last verse of every poem delivers a message that educates, enlightens, and empowers. Her searing signature endings find their way into your heart, open your mind to a deeper understanding, and stay with you forever.

©SharonEstherLampert.com

Be Born

Be Born.
Become Educated.
Love Your Work.
Make a Meaningful Contribution
To Yourself, Your Family, and Humanity.
Be a True Friend to Yourself First.
Have Sex with Someone You Love.
Make Love with Complete Abandon.
Enjoy Unconditional Love from Your Devoted Pet.
Make Time to Read the Funnies and Laugh.
Save Enough Money to Visit the Popular,
Pretty, and Peaceful Places of the World.
Read Great Literature, Listen to Great Music,
See Great Art, Watch the Great Movies,
Play the Fun Sports, Dance till Dawn,
Taste the Great Culinary Delights of the World -
Eat Slowly, Enjoy Every Bite, and Stay in Shape.
Plan One Great Adventure and Stick to the Plan.
Grow Old and Wise. Leave Your Money to Someone
You Love - Who Loves You Back.
Die in Your Sleep.

By Sharon Esther Lampert
Poet, Philosopher, Paladin of Education, Peacemaker, Pioneer, Prophet, and Princess
Book: **"I STOLE ALL THE WORDS FROM THE DICTIONARY"**
Email: **FANS@SharonEstherLampert.com**
www.SharonEstherLampert.com
www.PoetryJewels.com
www.WorldFamousPoems.com   ©All Rights Reserved. SharonEstherLampert.

The SOLE Intention of My Poetry Is to Add LIGHT to Your SOUL

WORLD PEACE EQUATION

VG+VL=VP
Virtue of the Good + Value of Life = Vision of Peace

The Mathematical and Philosophical Proof for World Peace

VG + VL = VP

VP = VG + VL

VP = V(G+L)

P = (G+L)

Peace = Good + Life

Peace = Goodlife

Sharon Esther Lampert
PEACEMAKER

Book: **"I STOLE ALL THE WORDS FROM THE DICTIONARY"**
Email: **FANS@SharonEstherLampert.com**

www.SharonEstherLampert.com
www.PoetryJewels.com
www.WorldFamousPoems.com
www.PhilosopherQueen.com   ©All Rights Reserved. SharonEstherLampert.

The SOLE Intention of My Poetry Is to Add LIGHT to Your SOUL

WORLD FAMOUS POEMS

THE 22 COMMANDMENTS

ALL YOU WILL EVER NEED TO KNOW ABOUT GOD
A UNIVERSAL MORAL COMPASS FOR ALL PEOPLE,
FOR ALL RELIGIONS, AND FOR ALL TIME

1. **LIFE** Over Death
2. **STRENGTH** Over Weakness
3. **DEED** Over Sin
4. **LOVE** Over Hatred
5. **TRUTH** Over Lie
6. **COURAGE** Over Fear
7. **OPTIMISM** Over Pessimism
8. **SHARING** Over Selfishness
9. **PRAISE** Over Criticism
10. **LOYALTY** Over Abandonment
11. **RESPONSIBILITY** Over Blame
12. **GRATITUDE** Over Envy
13. **REWARD** Over Punishment
14. **GENEROSITY** Over Stinginess
15. **CREATION** Over Destruction
16. **EDUCATION** Over Ignorance
17. **COOPERATION** Over Competition
18. **FREEDOM** Over Oppression
19. **COMPASSION** Over Indifference
20. **FORGIVENESS** Over Revenge
21. **PEACE** Over War
22. **JOY** Over Suffering

By Sharon Esther Lampert
Poet, Philosopher, Peacemaker, Prophet, Princess, Phoenix, and Prodigy
Book: **"I STOLE ALL THE WORDS FROM THE DICTIONARY"**
Email: **FANS@SharonEstherLampert.com**
www.SharonEstherLampert.com
www.PoetryJewels.com
www.WorldFamousPoems.com   ©All Rights Reserved. SharonEstherLampert.

The SOLE Intention of My Poetry Is to Add LIGHT to Your SOUL

Also By the Author

Critical Works in Poetry

"A List" As One of the World's Greatest Poets

#1 Poetry Website for Student Projects

Title: I Stole All the Words from the Dictionary
ISBN Hardcover: 978-1-885872-06-7
ISBN Paperback: 978-1-885872-07-4
ISBN E-Book: 978-1-885872-08-1
Website: www.SharonEstherLampert.com

Title: POETRY JEWELS: Diamonds, Emeralds, Sapphires, Rubies, and Pearls
ISBN Hardcover: 978-1-885872-15-9
ISBN Paperback: 978-1-885872-16-6
ISBN E-Book: 978-1-885872-17-3
Website: www.PoetryJewels.com

Title: V.E.S.S.E.L. VERY. EXTRA. SPECIAL. SHARON. ESTHER. LAMPERT.
ISBN Hardcover: 978-1-885872-09-8
ISBN Paperback: 978-1-885872-10-4
ISBN E-Book: 978-1-885872-11-1
Website: www.SharonEstherLampert.com

Title: SWEET NOTHINGS: 40 LOVE POEMS
ISBN Hardcover: 978-1-885872-30-2
ISBN Paperback: 978-1-885872-31-9
ISBN E-Book: 978-1-885872-32-6
Website: www.SharonEstherLampert.com

Critical Work in Theology

Title: THE 22 COMMANDMENTS: ALL YOU WILL EVER NEED TO KNOW ABOUT GOD
ISBN Hardcover: 978-1-885872-03-6
ISBN Paperback: 978-1-885872-04-3
ISBN E-Book: 978-1-885872-05-0
Website: www.SharonEstherLampert.com

Critical Work in Philosophy

Title: GOD OF WHAT? IS LIFE A GIFT OR A PUNISHMENT? 40 ABSOLUTE TRUTHS
ISBN Hardcover: 978-1-885872-00-5   **WORLD PREMIERE!**
ISBN Paperback: 978-1-885872-01-2
ISBN E-Book: 978-1-885872-02-9
Website: www.GodofWhat.com

Critical Work in Children's Literature - Color Coded Glossary
10 YEAR ANNIVERSARY EDITION

Title: SCHMALTZY: IN AMERICA, EVEN A CAT CAN HAVE A DREAM
ISBN Hardcover: 978-1-885872-39-5
ISBN Paperback: 978-1-885872-38-8
ISBN E-Book: 978-1-885872-37-1
Website: www.Schmaltzy.com

Critical Works in Literature

Title: 40 RULES OF MANHOOD - WORLD PREMIERE!
HOW DO SILLY LITTLE BOYS GROW INTO SANE BIG MEN
ISBN Hardcover: 978-1-885872-29-6
ISBN Paperback: 978-1-885872-35-7
ISBN E-Book: 978-1-885872-41-8
Website: www.SillyLittleBoys.com

Title: AMNON: THE HIDDEN WORLD OF SEX, ART, AND GENIUS
ISBN Hardcover: 978-1-885872-12-8
ISBN Paperback: 978-1-885872-13-5
ISBN E-Book: 978-1-885872-14-2
Website: www.SharonEstherLampert.com

Title: UNLEASH THE CREATOR THE GOD WITHIN - WORLD PREMIERE!
10 ESOTERIC LAWS OF GENIUS AND CREATIVITY
ISBN Hardcover: 978-1-885872-21-0
ISBN Paperback: 978-1-885872-22-7
ISBN E-Book: 978-1-885872-23-4
Website: www.SharonEstherLampert.com

Title: 10 MIRACLES: WHAT HAPPENS WHEN YOU FREE YOUR MIND OF NEGATIVITY?
ISBN Hardcover: 978-1-885872-33-3
ISBN Paperback: 978-1-885872-34-0
ISBN E-Book: 978-1-885872-36-4
Website: www.SharonEstherLampert.com

Turn One Night Stand into One True Love
10 YEAR ANNIVERSARY EDITION
Title: **SEX ON A PLATE: FOOD AS FOREPLAY**
THE COOKBOOK OF EVERLASTING LOVE
ISBN Hardcover: 978-1-885872-46-3
ISBN Paperback: 978-1-885872-48-7
ISBN E-Book: 978-1-885872-47-0
Website: www.TrueLoveBurnsEternal.com

The Only Thing You Have to Lose by Reading This Book Is Weight
Title: **WIN AT THIN**
ISBN Hardcover: 978-1-885872-24-1
ISBN Paperback: 978-1-885872-25-8
ISBN E-Book: 978-1-885872-26-5
Website: www.SharonEstherLampert.com

Critical Works in Education
SMARTGRADES BRAIN POWER REVOLUTION

Title: **THE SILENT CRISIS DESTROYING AMERICA'S BRIGHTEST MINDS**
BOOK OF THE MONTH: ALMA PUBLIC LIBRARY, WISCONSIN
ISBN Hardcover: 978-1-885872-52-5
ISBN Paperback: 978-1-885872-54-8
ISBN E-Book: 978-1-885872-53-1
Website: www.smartgrades.com

Title: **Your Study Room Is Under New Management**
ISBN Hardcover: 978-1-885872-79-1
ISBN Paperback: 978-1-885872-80-7
ISBN E-Book: 978-1-885872-81-4
Website: www.smartgrades.com

Title: **EVERY DAY AN EASY A - 3 EDITIONS (Elementary, High School, and College)**
ELE ISBN Hardcover: 978-1-885872-93-7
HS   ISBN Hardcover: 978-1-885872-95-1
COLLEGE   ISBN Hardcover: 978-1-885872-97-5
Website: www.everydayaneasya.com

Title: **TOTAL RECALL - 3 EDITIONS (Elementary, High School, and College)**
ELE   ISBN Hardcover: 978-1-885872-49-4
HS   ISBN Hardcover: 978-1-885872-50-0
COLLEGE   ISBN Hardcover: 978-1-885872-51-7
Website: www.smartgrades.com

FAN MAIL
FANS@SharonEstherLampert.com

A PHENOMENON...SHARON ESTHER LAMPERT

Lithe and lovely ... like a fawn.
This lady fascinates me ... from dusk till dawn.
Feminine and comely ... she's beyond belief
A blue-beam from her eyes ... is my soothing relief.

Girlish in her braces ... maidenly in her style
I yearn for her embraces ... and adore her friendly smile.
As tasteful as any artist ... you'll ever see
She's a compendium of class ... from A to Z.

If you'd like to see a figure, that puts Venus to shame
Behold her in a swimsuit, and your passions will aflame.
Ever exuding goodness ... guided from above
Miss Sharon is the essence, and epitome of Love.

She's the inspiration of sages, and also fools like me
And the most magnificent female, I'm sure I'll ever see.
The nights are now endearing, & never filled with doubt
I sometimes wake up singing, cause it's Sharon ...
I dream about.

Affectionately,..
A devoted fan,
Harry McVeety

Practice Gratitude — Count Your Blessings

Blessing 1. My Genetics & Gift of Genius — LEFTY
- Genetic Inheritance: Painter Grandfather Benjamin Paikoff & Sculptor Father Abraham Lampert
- Vocalist: Estelle Leibling, Chaim Frieberg, Ashira Orchestra, 18 Years: Ramaz Women's Service (YouTube)
- Athlete: "Faster Than Any Boy, Anytime, Anywhere, Any Age!"

Blessing 2. My Life at the Dawn of the Golden Age of the Digital Revolution
- APPLE: The Digital Revolution and APPLEISM "Steve JObs Is GOds"
- ADOBE: The Golden Age of Creativity
- INGRAM: The Golden Age of Publishing
- SOCIAL MEDIA: The Golden Age of the Internet & Global Communication
- iTUNES: The Golden Age of Music

Blessing 3. My Loved Ones and Muses, Boyfriends, Lovers, and Playdates
- Self-Love and Sanity: Practice Mindfulness, Meditation, and Music
- Unconditional Love: Mommy Eve Lampert
- My PURRfect Children: SCHMALTZY and FALAFEL (www.Schmaltzy.com)
- My Muses and N.Y.C. Night Life (Broadway Shows, Concerts, Restaurants)
- My Bubbe Esther Tulkoff (www.EstherTulkoff.com)

Blessing 4. My Education & Educators
- N.YU. B.A., M.A., M.A. and N.Y.U. Award for Multi-Interdisciplinary Studies (YouTube videos)
- N.Y.U. MENTOR: Laurin Raiken
- MY MUSE: Karl Bardosh "Friends First and Forever, and Family"
- Dave Segal: "Please don't let me DIE with a TYPO!
- Andy Anselmo: Voice Teacher "The Singer's Forum" N.Y.C.
- Cantor Sherwin Goffin of LSS & Riva Alper of the RAMAZ Women's Service (18 Years)
- Sandy Pione: Sports Coach, N.J. - Basketball and Softball

Blessing 5. My Sports
- N.Y.C. Marathon
- Basketball: N.Y.U. Women's Varsity Basketball Team, Center
- Basketball: N.Y.C. Urban Professional League
- Skiing: Heavenly, Lake Tahoe, Nevada
- Tennis: N.Y.C. Central Park Tennis Courts
- Weightlifting Contest Winner! N.Y.U. Coles Sports Center

Blessing 6. My Inspirations
- My Spiritual Ghost Companion (childhood-adult): Poet Hannah Senesh: "ELI, ELI"
- DEEP I: Eckhart Tolle (Painbody, Presence, and Power of Now!)
- ICON: Supreme Court Justice Ruth Bader Ginsburg (Lefty)
- ISRAEL: "AM YISRAEL CHAI!" (LAMBS to SLAUGHTER to LIONS to LIGHT of the WORLD)

What Do Books Do?

BOOKS ARE POWERFUL!

Books Educate!
Books Enlighten!
Books Empower!
Books Entertain!
Books Emancipate!
Books Spring Eternal!
Books Drive Exploration!
Books Spark Evolution!
Books Ignite Revolution!

Philosopher-Queen-Prodigy Sharon Esther Lampert

KADIMAH PRESS
Gifts of Genius

My Books Are My Remains
Please Handle Them Gently

Sharon Esther Lampert
Prodigy, Poet, Philosopher, Prophet, Peacemaker, Prophet, Phoenix

www.ingramcontent.com/pod-product-compliance
Lightning Source LLC
Chambersburg PA
CBHW042246100526
44587CB00002B/43